Summary and Findings
of the
National Supported Work Demonstration

Summary and Findings of the National Supported Work Demonstration

The Board of Directors
Manpower Demonstration Research Corporation

Ballinger Publishing Company ● Cambridge, Massachusetts
A Subsidiary of Harper & Row, Publishers, Inc.

International Standard Book Number: 0-88410-687-X (hardcover)
0-88410-688-8 (paperback)

Library of Congress Catalog Card Number: 80-12202

Printed in the United States of America

Library of Congress Cataloging in Publication Data

Manpower Demonstration Research Corporation.
  Board of Directors.
  Summary and findings of the national supported work demonstration.

  1. Hard-core unemployment—United States. 2. Manpower policy—United States. 3. Manpower Demonstration Research Corporation. I. Title.
HD5724.M2387   1980   331.13'77'0973   80-12202
ISBN 0-88410-687-X
ISBN 0-88410-688-8 (pbk.)

This book was written and prepared by the staff and Board of Directors of the Manpower Demonstration Research Corporation as part of the final report on the National Supported Work Demonstration, which was funded by the following grants or contracts:

Employment and Training Administration
Department of Labor
(Grant No. 33-36-75-01)

Employment and Training Administration
Department of Labor
(Contract Nos. 30-36-75-01 and 30-34-75-02)

The Ford Foundation
(Grant No. 740-0537A)

The Employment and Training Administration of the Department of Labor is the lead agency in a federal funding consortium, which includes the following additional agencies:

Law Enforcement Assistance Administration
U.S. Department of Justice

Office of Planning and Evaluation
U.S. Department of Health, Education and Welfare

National Institute on Drug Abuse
U.S. Department of Health, Education and Welfare

Office of Policy Research and Development
U.S. Department of Housing and Urban Development

Office of Community Action
U.S. Community Services Administration

The Economic Development Administration
U.S. Department of Commerce

The points of view or opinions stated in this document are not intended to represent the official position or policy of the supporting funding agencies.

Acknowledgments

While this summary report carries the Board of Directors as the author, the Board concentrated on preparing the first section on Findings and Recommendations. Members of the MDRC staff were primarily responsible for the preparation of the nine chapters which make up the body of the book. Judith Gueron was the principal author, assisted by Gary Walker and Andrew Solomon. William Grinker contributed a critical review of the entire draft. Acknowledgment is also made to Karen Paget, who supervised the compilation of data and preparation of tables, and to Sheila Mandel, who coordinated production. Special appreciation is expressed to Robert Goldmann of the Ford Foundation, who provided valuable editorial advice and assistance.

In turn, MDRC relied heavily on the input of its major research contractor, Mathematica Policy Research, in particular, on Robinson Hollister, Rebecca Maynard, and Valerie Leach. The report also draws on the work of Peter Kemper, Craig Thornton, and David Long of Mathematica Policy Research and of Stanley Masters, Katherine Dickinson, and Irving Piliavin at the Institute for Research on Poverty, University of Wisconsin, Madison, a principal subcontractor on the research.

Table of Contents

List of Tables

List of Figures

Summary and Findings
of the
National Supported Work Demonstration

Findings and Recommendations

The Board of Directors of the Manpower Demonstration Research Corporation submits for the consideration of its funding agencies, and of other groups concerned with the use of employment and training programs to assist hard-to-employ persons, the following findings and recommendations. This report results from a 5-year demonstration and research effort on supported work.

SUMMARY OF FINDINGS

The supported work program provides individuals with severe employment problems with work experience of a year or so, under conditions of gradually increasing demands, close supervision, and work in association with a crew of peers. The four hard-to-employ groups on whom the program concentrates are women on Aid to Families with Dependent Children (AFDC) for many years; ex-addicts; ex-offenders; and young school dropouts, often with criminal records or histories of delinquency. The guiding principle of the supported work experiment is that by participating in the program, a significant number of people who are severely handicapped for employment may be able to join the labor force and do productive work, cease engaging in socially destructive or dependent behavior, and become self-supporting members of society.

To place supported work into the perspective of national manpower programs, it must be noted that it was a demonstration-research effort rather than a broad, comprehensive program; that its 5-year cost of $82.4 million represented about one-tenth of one percent of the total that the U.S. federal government has spent on manpower since 1962; and that it had limited objectives.

Given its experimental purpose, and given the severe handicaps of the groups to whom it addressed itself, the supported work program was not expected to be successful with all or even a majority of its target groups. However, one of the research aims was to learn which group benefited more, which less, and which not at all. The destructiveness of poverty, poor education, discrimination, and high unemployment cannot be expected to yield entirely to an employment intervention of a year's duration. But it was possible, so the initial hypothesis held, that an investment of $5,000 to $8,000 per person might yield good enough results for a sufficient number of these individuals to justify the expenditure. This hypothesis took into account not only the high cost of long-term transfer payments for some of these individuals, but also the fact that the criminal and other antisocial behavior of ex-addicts, ex-offenders, and delinquent youths often entails serious costs to society other than dollars.

Rather than recommending the early launching of yet another national manpower program with multibillion-dollar appropriations, the planners of supported work decided to make a careful test of the concept, and to conduct rigorous research on its application free from the pressure of producing the immediate results which a full-scale national program normally demands. After 5 years, these are the highlights of the results.

The program has proved most effective in preparing for employment a substantial number of women who have been on welfare (AFDC) for many years. This is important in view of the large number of women in this category and their dependence on public assistance.

The program also has had an impact on a significant segment of the ex-addict population, who did better in getting jobs and in earnings than members of a control group who were not in the program. In addition, the ex-addicts in the program were less likely to commit drug-related and other crimes than those who were not.

The program had a marginal impact on ex-offenders, who did not show less criminal behavior, and whose rate of employment and earnings was only slightly better than those of ex-offenders who did not participate.

The program did not yield long-term positive results for the youth group.

Before further detailing these findings, it is necessary to describe the key characteristics of the program and the processes through which it produced its results.

KEY FEATURES, ORIGIN, AND MANAGEMENT OF THE PROGRAM

The supported work experiment was characterized by a number of special features not common to other employment programs, as well as by a rigorously designed and implemented research effort. The local programs were operated by nonprofit organizations, which were responsible for hiring the participants, all of whom volunteered, and for developing and supervising worksites. For the most part, persons enrolled in supported work were assigned to a work crew composed of a small number of individuals like themselves, usually 10 or less, with a supervisor who was able to serve as foreman and counselor-helper to assist those who were first becoming exposed to the demands and discipline of the work setting. During the final phases of what was up to 12 months of employment, the local operators assisted the supported workers in finding a job.

Each supported work program had a range of different worksites including construction work, such as rehabilitating old houses; small manufacturing operations involving recapping tires or building furniture; or activities like managing a public park or operating a day-care center. Special efforts were made to involve the private sector and to ensure the cooperation of organized labor. Revenues from the sale of goods and services produced by the work crews helped finance the programs; in addition, waivers were obtained through the Department of Health, Education and Welfare (HEW) to permit welfare allowances to be converted into wages for the participants.

To operate the complex program, a national management organization, the Manpower Demonstration Research Corporation (MDRC), was set up to oversee both operations and the research effort. MDRC was organized in 1974 as a nonprofit organization with the assistance and encouragement of the agencies that decided to fund the supported work effort—the U.S. Department of Labor, the U.S. Department of Health, Education and Welfare, the U.S. Department of Justice, the U.S. Department of Housing and Urban Development, and the Ford Foundation. The members of the Board of Directors, originally an advisory committee to the funding agencies to explore the feasibility of the project and to advise on its design, have been directly and continuously involved in every phase of the demonstration.

Early in the exploration, a consensus was reached among the senior officials of the funding agencies and members of the Advisory Board that the key requirement for the effective conduct of the supported work demonstration was a major research effort integrated into the basic program structure. Only in that way could reliable information be developed about the program's performance and its potential contribution in shaping national employment and social policy. Too many costly federal programs had been established and expanded without adequate information about their effectiveness. Supported work sought to change this process: to acquire knowledge before legislators had to decide whether a demonstration should be expanded into a national program.

The supported work demonstration was conducted at 15 sites, 10 of which were utilized for research on the impact of the program and its benefit and costs. This research was carried out by Mathematica Policy Research and the Institute for Research on Poverty at the University of Wisconsin. All 15 local operations were covered by another phase of research—the documentation of operations at individual sites—by MDRC staff and consultants. The maximum number of participants at any one site was 300. Altogether, 10,043 persons were enrolled during the demonstration period.

Strict eligibility criteria were set to limit participation to individuals who had severe handicaps in obtaining employment and who, in fact, had little recent work experience. Most enrollees were black or Hispanic (over 90 percent except in the case of ex-addicts); less than one-third had graduated from high school (the youth group was composed exclusively of high school dropouts); and less than one-quarter were married. The number of weeks worked during the preceding 12 months averaged between 3 and 10; and except for the AFDC group, the arrest rates for the other three groups ranged from a low of 54 percent to a high of 100 percent, with heavy drug use (heroin) characteristic of the ex-offenders as well as the ex-addicts. Except for AFDC participants, most supported workers were male.

All enrollees were volunteers. The principle of random assignment was followed in selecting one person to participate, the other as a control. A total of 6,616 individuals made up the research sample for the impact study; 3,214 were participants and 3,402 were controls.

Each person in the sample received a baseline interview and up to four successive interviews at 9-month intervals. Information collected in the interviews was checked for accuracy against appropriate social security, welfare, and criminal justice records.

Expenditures for the demonstration—including public, philanthropic, and private sector funds—amounted to $82.4 million, of which about $11 million represent the costs of research. The full exploitation of the findings of this extensive research effort is constrained by the dearth of adequate information from most of the other federally financed manpower programs operated since 1962. These include institutional training, on-the-job training, the Job Corps, the Neighborhood Youth Corps, Public Service Employment, work experience programs, and the Work Incentive (WIN) Program. Because they were not structured to yield reliable cost and outcome data, comparisons between these other programs and supported work are difficult and sometimes impossible. However, as more detailed supported work reports become available during 1980, program designers and operators will be able to use the information from the supported work experiment to illuminate issues in other manpower programs.

The supported work research effort yielded extensive data on the costs and benefits of the program. Detailed financial data were available, and the control group methodology produced reliable information about the program's impact. Still, cost-benefit analysis requires a good many assumptions and judgments, and in some categories, the figures are imprecise. These include the value of the output that the supported workers produced while in the program; the social benefits of reduced crime; the discount rate used in calculating the present value of future benefits and costs; and the extent to which benefits registered for that part of the sample who were interviewed through the final survey of 27 and 36 months could be generalized for the rest of the sample or projected into the future.

In making its cost-benefit estimates, the Board was guided by experience from current social science research and selected middle-of-the-range values. In a later chapter, and in more detailed reports that follow, a range of estimates is presented that will enable those interested to calculate the net benefits on the basis of alternative assumptions.

Still, some data have not been fully mined, and additional analyses remain to be done. But rather than wait for the completion of all the subsidiary research tasks—and these are going forward currently—the Board has decided to report the key findings now that the basic analyses have been completed.

RESULTS BY TARGET GROUP

The AFDC Group
To be eligible for the program, a person had to be female, on AFDC for 30 of the last 36 months, and with no children under 6

years of age. She had to meet the demonstration-wide requirements of being currently unemployed and with only limited recent work experience. AFDC recipients meeting these criteria constitute about 15 percent of the total AFDC population.

The average age of AFDC participants was 34; all but 5 percent were black or Hispanic; less than one-third were high school graduates; only 3 percent were currently married; and the average number of dependents in the household was 2.2; 14 percent had never worked, and an additional 61 percent had not held a full-time job during the last 2 years; their earnings during the past year averaged $240 and their stay on welfare averaged over 8.5 years.

Here are the results for this group:

1.   **Supported work has proved to be an effective program to enhance the employability and earnings of long-term AFDC recipients and to reduce their dependence on welfare payments.** This finding emerged from the research data showing that the AFDC women who participated in the program performed significantly better than the controls in terms of increased employment, increased earnings and reduced welfare dependence. The significance of these differentials has held up consistently throughout the post-program period, as reflected in interviews over 27 months.

Preliminary analysis of additional data indicates that supported work appears to be most effective for AFDC recipients with the least prior work experience.

2.   **Many of the AFDC group sought and obtained jobs and remained employed even though their earnings were substantially offset by loss of welfare benefits.** Many female heads of household are willing to work for very small financial gains in preference to the social opprobrium of continuing on welfare and suffering the governmental interference in their lives associated with being on public assistance.

3.   **The cost-benefit calculation for the AFDC group reveals that, primarily because of the employment and earnings gains of participants after they leave the program and because of the value of the goods and services produced by them while they are in supported work, the net benefit to society is considerable.** Moreover, the benefits to the taxpayer from reductions in welfare payments, the taxes paid on earnings, and the reduced use of food stamps, housing subsidies, and Medicaid exceed the cost of providing the supported work jobs.

4.   **The average stay in the program of AFDC participants was about 9.5 months—longer than that of any other target group.** This is attributable to the reluctance of these participants to leave sup-

ported work for jobs in the labor market and to the difficulty that local programs encountered in their search for suitable employers willing to hire supported work participants. Almost 25 percent of the AFDC group could not obtain or would not accept a regular job at the completion of their maximum period of employment.

5. **Preliminary indications are that supported work has the greatest impact in periods of high unemployment, possibly because in such circumstances employers are less inclined to hire "risky" workers (those with little or no work experience).** This gives supported work participants, with their recent and structured experience in a work program, an advantage over their control group counterparts.

The Ex-Addict Group

Ex-addicts—both participants and the control group—were selected from those participating in a drug treatment program at the time of enrollment or within the preceding 6 months. Almost all had used heroin. Four out of 5 were male, with an average age of 28 years; 6 out of 7 were black or Hispanic; less than 29 percent were high school graduates; just under 1 out of 4 was currently married; 5 percent had never worked and an additional one-third had not held a full-time job during the preceding 24 months. On average, they had worked 10 weeks during the past year, earning about $1,230; 2 out of 5 had received welfare payments in the month prior to enrollment; 9 out of 10 had been arrested; and on the average they had spent 129 weeks in jail.

Here are the results:

6. **During and after the time when the ex-addicts were in the supported work program, they were involved in substantially less criminal activity than the control group.** The Board notes that this impact of supported work on the ex-addicts is unusual among interventions aimed at ex-addicts, many of whom have reverted to crime to pay for their drugs after participating in other types of programs.

7. **For the sample followed the full 36 months, the data suggest that supported work resulted in an improvement in the employment and earnings figures of experimentals over controls that grew in the period between the 27th and 36th month, after having narrowed perceptibly in the post-program period up to 27 months.** The reversal in the differentials that set in after 27 months appears to reflect the delay that many ex-addicts experienced in finding employment after leaving the supported work program. The delayed

start on the job may be related to the fact that many ex-addicts were eligible for unemployment insurance.

8. The benefits of the program exceed the costs for ex-addicts when the gains from a reduction in destructive behavior, especially drug-related and other criminal offenses, are added to those resulting from increased employment and earnings and from the value of the products of the supported workers while they are in the program.

The Ex-Offender Group

Eligibility for the ex-offender group required an individual to have been incarcerated as a result of a conviction within the last 6 months; 19 out of 20 were males, and over 90 percent were black or Hispanic. The average age was 25 years. About 1 in 4 had completed 12 or more years of school; 1 in 8 was married, 11 percent reported that they had never worked, and an additional 39 percent had not worked at a full-time job during the preceding 24 months. They had worked an average of less than 6 weeks during the preceding year and had earned $580. In the month before enrollment, 17 percent had received welfare payments. About one-third reported that they were regular users of heroin. The average number of arrests per participant was over 9, with previous time in jail averaging almost 200 weeks.

Here are the results:

9. Although supported work participants had a somewhat better employment and earnings record after 27 months than the control group, the difference was not statistically significant. And, unlike the ex-addicts, the ex-offenders who had participated in the program did not show any reduction in criminal behavior.

10. The costs and benefits for the ex-offender group vary so widely depending on the assumptions used, that the Board at this stage cannot arrive at a clear-cut finding. It is possible that further research, particularly if it reveals a continuation of the employment and earnings differentials between the experimentals and the controls, may point to a positive outcome.

11. Ex-offenders dropped out from the program at a relatively high rate. Their average length of stay was 5.2 months. This finding most likely reflects unmet expectations with regard to work assignments, work settings, and wages, especially in comparison to the returns from criminal activity. Perhaps most important was the uncertainty of this group that, after completing the program the members could find a permanent job and thereby have the option of breaking away from a life of crime.

The Youth Group

Eligibility was limited to young people between the ages of 17 and 20 years who had dropped out of school, with 1 out of every 2 enrollees required to have a record of delinquency or crime.

Males outnumbered females in the ratio of 6 to 1. Only 6 percent of the group were white. Their average age was slightly above 18 years. Less than 4 percent were married. Over 20 percent had never worked. On the average, they had been employed for 9 weeks during the preceding year and had earned $827. About 1 in 8 had received welfare in the month prior to enrolling in the program. More than half had been arrested.

Here are the results:

12. **Supported work had no significant long-term impact on the earnings, employment, criminal activity or drug abuse of the youth group. The program's benefits for youth fell short of its costs.** The data do suggest, however, that the younger segment of the youth group benefit more from the program than do older participants. Many youths find it difficult to decide what kind of work to do and, when they do, to carry out their plans. Thus, they tend to seek short-term experiences, either in or out of work, and many quickly tire of their jobs. This attitude makes the discipline and routine of supported work unattractive to them. Moreover, their realization that the program will at best prepare them for an uncertain opportunity for an entry-level job or a career is another negative factor.

MDRC is currently conducting a modified supported work program for youths at several sites. It includes these additional elements: remedial education, skill training, and support services. It is possible that this, or a similarly enriched model of supported work may prove more effective for certain youth groups than standard training or employment programs.

FINDINGS ON MANAGEMENT AND IMPLICATIONS FOR EXPANSION

Supported work programs were operated by 15 independent local organizations. MDRC entered into yearly performance contracts with these local operators, monitored their activities, offered technical assistance, and with the Department of Labor's approval, expanded, contracted, closed down, or made appropriate management changes based on program performance. Under this charge, one site was closed and several with serious problems were reorganized. Half of the resources for program operations were provided by the national funding consortium, with the rest from locally allocated grants, the majority of which came from local CETA agencies; welfare payments converted into wage payments with the approval of HEW and by agreement with local welfare agencies; and revenues derived from the sale of goods or services produced by supported workers. MDRC was responsible for the allocation of the national funding and oversight of all of these resources.

This meant that MDRC had to shape a single program funded by agencies with different guidelines, different objectives, and different operating styles, and to speak with one voice on the local level, where the programs were being operated. Out of this experience the Board has derived certain management lessons:

13. **The establishment or use of a nonprofit intermediary such as MDRC greatly facilitates the ability of government agencies to pursue a common objective and to harness governmental and philanthropic support to an agreed social goal.** The federal agencies found in MDRC a vehicle for managing both the multiple funding and the operations of a program that might otherwise not have been launched.

14. **Multiple sponsorship and financial support at the national level was paralleled at the local level by the complexity of program operations that required a variety of training and financial and technical assistance.** MDRC supplied this assistance, seeking to maintain a balance between local creativity and distinctiveness, and the need for adherence to demonstration-wide criteria essential for maintaining program integrity and conducting a national research program.

15. **Important to the implementation of supported work are (a) the development of a broad range of worksite activities within each operating program including clerical, human services, production of goods and construction, with a mix of public and private customers; and (b) relatively intensive worksite supervision, crew work, and a careful structuring of demands and rewards to facilitate the gradual development of participants' skills and expectations.**

16. **Experience in managing the national demonstration has convinced the Board that effective implementation of the supported work model requires a staged and closely monitored approach.** To expand the program massively and quickly would jeopardize the adherence to basic guidelines and criteria, outpace available technical assistance resources, and place excessive burdens on management information systems. These resources are the heart of an effective program; and expansion plans should assure that these resources

are available, both in quantity and quality, to meet the demands of program growth.

17. During the demonstration period, the supported work programs were implemented by local, nonprofit organizations. However, subsequent experience suggests that under certain conditions, they can also be implemented through the CETA system. This requires that the CETA regulations allow sufficient flexibility so that programs can meet the needs of supported work participants, who are often considerably more disadvantaged and therefore a more difficult challenge to operators than regular CETA enrollees. It also requires that there be a centralized management organization available to provide supplemental funding, technical assistance, and guidance in implementing the supported work model.

RECOMMENDATIONS

Based on the above findings, the Board of the Manpower Demonstration Research Corporation makes these recommendations.

1. Immediate action should be taken to launch new or expanded supported work programs for AFDC mothers and former drug abusers in interested communities, and to do so in close cooperation with the CETA, WIN and drug-abuse treatment systems. Cost-benefit analyses clearly point in that direction. The new or expanded programs should be implemented in a carefully designed and phased manner, consistent with national management and information needs and capacities.

2. Even where the cost-benefit ratios are equivocal or unfavorable, as is the case with the ex-offender and youth groups, continuation of a modified type of supported work may, in the absence of demonstrably better alternatives, be a viable intervention strategy. The findings of surveys show that the American people firmly believe that employable persons ought to work rather than live off one or another form of income transfer. The use of supported work for these hard-to-employ groups must be assessed in the context of the other options available to them.

3. The Secretary of Labor should (a) seek, in 1980, an amendment to the CETA legislation that would establish supported work as a national program, (b) request funding to double the size of supported work and to cover costs not available from local sources and from the sale of goods and services produced by supported work enrollees, and (c) move to establish an appropriate instrumentality, either within an existing nonprofit organization or one es-

pecially created for that purpose, to work with prime sponsors and to assume the oversight and management responsibilities carried out so far by the Manpower Demonstration Research Corporation. The management information and fiscal systems currently being utilized by MDRC would be available to any such successor organization and would facilitate the transition to an ongoing national program.

4. **The Secretary of Health and Human Services should seek legislative authority to allow the diversion of welfare allowances into wages for an expanded supported work program.** The marked success of the AFDC group and the fact that the diversion of welfare allowances accounted for half of all supported work wages to this group points to the desirability of this recommendation which should be limited to persons on AFDC who volunteer for work.

5. **Provision should be made to continue on a selective basis research on the supported work program so as fully to exploit the data that were produced by the demonstration.** This should include a further limited follow-up effort to determine the longer term impact of the program on employment, earnings, and criminal activities. The research design and the extensive records that are available make it possible to do this.

6. **The potential of supported work for new groups, such as the mentally retarded, former mental patients, and other hard-to-employ groups, should be assessed and, where appropriate, implemented as part of an expanded supported work program.**

7. **The demonstration techniques that have proved themselves in supported work, coupled with a rigorously applied experimental research methodology and supported by a strong management information system, should be utilized in the future.** They offer an effective strategy to gain knowledge about the potential and the limitations of promising social programs, and they should be brought into play before policy-makers move to enter upon large-scale national replication.

Chapter 1

Introduction

The nation faces few problems as formidable as the presence of a group of people, largely concentrated in its principle cities, who live at the margin of society. Whether because of distortions in the economy, lack of training or motivation, or the attitudes of employers, these people have been excluded from the regular labor market and find, at most, sporadic employment. Though relatively few in number, they have become a considerable burden to themselves and the public—as long-term recipients of welfare, and as the source of much violent crime and drug addiction. They are simultaneously the source and the victims of urban decay.

To provide a bridge for these men and women to the labor market and to society, the supported work program was developed. It is a highly structured, transitional work experience that recognizes the need of these men and women, at least temporarily, for a work environment that is more supportive and more closely supervised than work normally is. It is a voluntary program that offers a temporary, subsidized job (generally for 12 months) in such an environment, in an atmosphere where participants can acquire the skills, habits, and credentials necessary to find and hold permanent, unsubsidized employment. Supported work thus seeks to accomplish several related objectives: to prepare people for the regular labor market; to produce marketable goods and services; and to reduce unemployment, welfare dependency, criminal behavior, and drug abuse. It aims to redistribute income through work rather than through welfare and other transfer payments.

For 5 years, supported work was operated as a rigorously controlled demonstration, designed to test the usefulness of the concept. Its objective was neither to create a new all-purpose antipoverty program, nor to serve as a pilot effort for general welfare reform or as a guaranteed jobs program. Instead, the purpose was to test the feasibility and impact of a tightly designed employment program. Previous social experiments tested alternative support systems, such as restructured welfare payments or housing subsidies; the supported work demonstration was the first major effort to test an employment program by means of a set of complex yet sharply defined experimental methods, built around the random assignment of applicants to experimental (participant) and control (comparison) groups. In many respects it was therefore also a demonstration of the feasibility of running a large and complex operating program under the controlled conditions of a social experiment.

Four hard-to-employ groups were chosen as participants in the national demonstration. The common denominator was little or no recent work experience. The four groups emerged from a process of discussion among the demonstration's planners, who sought to apply the supported work principle to individuals with some of the most serious handicaps to employment in the open labor market: female long-term recipients of welfare payments under the Aid to Families with Dependent Children (AFDC) program; ex-offenders recently released from prison; former drug addicts recently in treatment; and young school dropouts, half of whom had to have records of delinquency.

Fifteen separate nonprofit corporations, located throughout the nation, were selected or developed to operate supported work projects at the local level. In their own small factories and work crews, as well as in public or private sector jobs in the labor market, these local operators attempted to apply the supported work model in their own economic, political, and administrative settings. Conflicts naturally emerged between the researcher's desire for standardization and the program operator's need for flexibility to adapt supported work to local conditions. Compromises were made. Some factors, such as eligibility criteria, wage rates, and program duration, had to be rigidly standardized and adhered to across all sites. Others, such as types of work and sources of local funds, were permitted to vary.

In all sites, however, every effort was made to maintain the integrity of the basic program design and to apply it. Supervisor-to-participant ratios were kept at a level that enabled the supervisors— who also had to serve as teachers, trouble-shooters, and role models—

to give individual attention to each participant. Care was taken not to overwhelm the new arrival with performance demands. Instead, standards of attendance, punctuality, and productivity were gradually but steadily increased until they approached or equaled those demanded in the regular labor market. In the language of the demonstration, this supported work feature was called "graduated stress." Finally, emphasis was placed on crew work and peer group support. A participant worked among people who shared the same problems, in an environment where he or she did not have to feel isolated, or meet hostility or suspicion.

Preliminary planning and overall funding was supplied by a consortium of six federal agencies with interests in various aspects of the demonstration and the Ford Foundation. The six original agencies were:

The Employment and Training Administration
U.S. Department of Labor

The Law Enforcement Assistance Administration
U.S. Department of Justice

The National Institute on Drug Abuse
U.S. Department of Health, Education and Welfare

The Office of the Assistant Secretary for Planning and Education
U.S. Department of Health, Education and Welfare

The Office of Policy Research and Development
U.S. Department of Housing and Urban Development

The Economic Development Administration
U.S. Department of Commerce

The Employment and Training Administration of the Department of Labor served as the lead federal agency.

Early in the planning stage, the funding agencies decided that in order to coordinate the demonstration on behalf of all these sponsors and funding sources, as well as to maintain the basic features of the design throughout the different local sites, a single institution was needed to which all parties could turn and where responsibility for management could be located. Thus, they joined in creating the Manpower Demonstration Research Corporation (MDRC), a non-profit corporation, to undertake these central and fundamental tasks: to be the channel to the local supported work programs for funding agency support; to provide those programs with technical assistance; and, most importantly, to monitor and assess local program performance from both operational and research perspectives and to ensure the maintenance and application of the demonstration's basic operational and research designs.

The Board of Directors of this intermediary corporation was made up of men and women with extensive experience in social research and policy development. Before the new corporation was formed, several of its members had served as an advisory committee to the funding agencies. This committee was involved in developing the demonstration's research design; determining the balance between the demands of research and those of operations; making certain that research focused on key policy issues; and selecting the target groups for the demonstration. When MDRC was formed, the advisors became the nucleus of the organization's Board of Directors and were joined by additional members. The Board since those early days has been continuously and actively involved in guiding and reviewing the research effort and in shaping operational policy.

The funding agencies have also participated actively by providing advice and facilitating the progress of the demonstration. Representatives from these agencies regularly attended MDRC Board meetings and, less formally, were helpful in matters involving federal regulations and congressional relations and, in a variety of other ways, supported and assisted the MDRC staff. The cooperation between the funding agencies has been outstanding, particularly because each has had its own interests and research priorities.

Though the administrative and funding structures for the national supported work demonstration were in many respects unprecedented, the supported work concept itself was not original. The basic model was an outgrowth of two older social initiatives: the sheltered workshop, a program pioneered in Britain, the Netherlands, and Sweden designed to provide permanent subsidized employment and a sense of accomplishment to the physically and mentally handicapped; and the various American manpower efforts that have offered subsidized training and transitional jobs to the unemployed.

In the United States, these features were adapted and fused in a program that was developed by the Vera Institute of Justice in New

York City in 1972. Serving a population of ex-addicts, the program, to which Vera gave the name supported work, was well received during its first year of operation. In light of promising early findings, the program's sponsors were eager to see if the results could be replicated in other cities or with other target populations. Supported work also attracted the interest of a growing number of social scientists and professionals in the field of social policy, who saw regular productive employment as an effective remedy or "therapy" for many disadvantaged people in the United States.

There was yet another factor that played an important role in the launching of the national supported work demonstration. Beginning in the late 1960s, there was increasing dissatisfaction with the way in which many of the era's social programs had been implemented. New ideas had been too hurriedly translated into national programs and then, just as quickly, pronounced failures—all without the benefit of reliable information about what actually had occurred. Supported work offered an opportunity to institute a fresh approach. Tested as a pilot program by Vera, supported work could be expanded to operate as a large experiment with a comprehensive, rigorous research component that could tell funders, policy-makers, and the public what kinds of impact could be achieved with this approach, as well as what could not or could only inadequately be done. Only later, with the insights yielded by the research, would the concept be considered for wider implementation. It was on this moderate and, it was hoped, realistic research objective that the national funding consortium found itself in agreement.

Formal planning for the demonstration began in January 1974, with a conference involving 175 representatives from funding agencies, potential local program operators, and officials from states and localities. From 40 proposals submitted, 19 were accepted for 6-month planning grants, beginning in June 1974. At the conclusion of the planning period, 13 sites were selected for the demonstration. These sites began program operation between March and July 1975. In 1976, 2 more sites were added, bringing the total in the demonstration to 15. During the period of the demonstration, 1 site was terminated for inadequate performance. By the end of the 4-year demonstration period, over 10,000 men and women had participated in supported work, making the program one of the largest social experiments ever conducted in the United States.

The demonstration sought to answer five basic questions:

1. How effective is the model in increasing the long-term employ-

ment and earnings of participants, and in reducing welfare dependency, criminal activities, or drug abuse?
2. What target populations benefit most from supported work?
3. What does the program cost? To what extent does it produce valuable goods and services? How do the program's costs compare to its measurable benefits?
4. What local conditions, administrative auspices, and implementation strategies seem to be the most conducive to program success?
5. What particular characteristics of the program model have the greatest impact on individual performance and behavior?

The research effort was divided into three components: (1) the behavioral analysis; (2) the benefit-cost analysis; and (3) the process/documentation analysis. The behavioral analysis sought to measure the short- and long-term impact of the demonstration on the employment, income, drug use, and criminal behavior of the participants. At 10 of the 15 local sites, applicants to the program were randomly assigned to experimental (participant) and control (nonparticipating, comparison) groups. Interviews with members of both groups, conducted at 9-month intervals for up to 3 years, supplied the basic data for this analysis. Program impact was determined by a comparison of the behavior and experience of the experimentals with that of the controls.

The benefit-cost analysis sought to evaluate the net benefits (or costs) of supported work in economic terms. The demonstration was assessed from three perspectives: that of society in general; that of the actual participants; and that of people who do not participate (i.e., the taxpayers). The analysis drew its information from several sources: the interviews with experimentals and controls; a detailed study of the value of the goods and services produced; the MDRC fiscal and management information systems; and published estimates of the costs of crime and of drug treatment and other service programs.

The process/documentation analysis attempted to determine what program features not covered in the other two research components were associated with a project's success or failure. It involved a statistical effort to discover the interrelationships between the various program elements and participants' behavior both in and after leaving supported work, as well as a qualitative assessment of variables in the local projects. These included differences in the quality of leadership; types of job creation, placement and funding strategies; and the geographic, economic, and political environment in which the program operated. The statistical effort depended upon information from the research interviews and MDRC's supported work management information system. The qualitative assessment was based on the observations of MDRC research, Supported Work Management Information System (MIS), and operations staff, and on the work of several consultants.

Although MDRC had overall responsibility for supervising and directing the research, it subcontracted the behavioral, benefit-cost, and statistical process analyses to Mathematica Policy Research and the Institute for Research on Poverty, University of Wisconsin.

From the inception of the planning for the demonstration, the Board had developed a policy to assure that the rights of those individuals being followed by the research would be protected. Subsequently, the Department of Health, Education and Welfare developed regulations concerning the protection of human subjects that extended to social science experiments. As a result, the Board's earlier planning was adapted to these regulations, and an Institutional Review Board was established to oversee the supported work demonstration. This group examined the extent to which the project put individuals at risk, proposed safeguards to protect them, and sought to balance the potential research benefits against the risks. The Institutional Review Board focused its attention on the problems posed by the collection of highly confidential information (especially that on illegal activities), the possible risks to the youths and AFDC women following their association with ex-offenders and ex-addicts, and the psychological risks of random assignment. This led to the adoption of extensive procedures to inform participants and controls about the demonstration, and to limit access to the research data.

The total cost of the 4-year demonstration and the 5-year research effort was $82.4 million, of which $49.5 million came from the national funding partners; $32.9 million was raised locally by the program operators from the sale of goods and services, from locally generated grants, or from a diversion of AFDC benefits that allowed funds that would have been paid out as welfare benefits to be used instead to pay part of the AFDC supported workers' wages. A total of $66.4 million was spent on local program operations, with the remaining expenditures covering research, monitoring and technical assistance, and the operation of the demonstration's fiscal and management information system.

This general report is the first in a series of final reports on the demonstration. Specific target group analyses, the complete benefit-cost report, process/documentation studies, and technical documentation papers will be available in the near future. Chapter 2 discusses the implementation of the demonstration on the local level. Chapter 3 deals with the research strategy, while Chapters 4 through 7 report the findings for each target group. The results of the benefit-cost analysis are summarized in Chapter 8, and Chapter 9 summarizes and assesses the overall findings.

Implementing the Demonstration

The design of the supported work demonstration was developed by the Manpower Demonstration Research Corporation (MDRC) Board of Directors, staff, and subcontractors in conjunction with the federal funding agencies. MDRC was responsible for ongoing management and oversight of the research and local supported work program operations. Local supported work programs were conducted by independent agencies operating under performance contracts with MDRC. Supported workers were employees of these agencies, which were responsible for developing and operating worksites, supplying equipment, hiring supervisors, and eventually assisting supported workers in finding nonsubsidized jobs when they left the program. These agencies represented a variety of geographic and economic conditions and administrative auspices, as shown in Table 2-1.

The basic structure—locally run programs following a national design and overseen by a national agency—set up a tension that was inherent to the demonstration. On the one hand, there was the necessity to establish and enforce uniform design and performance standards in order to maintain program integrity. On the other hand, local operators had to be provided with the flexibility to deal with constraints and to take advantage of opportunities in their widely differing communities. MDRC sought to sustain and balance both aspects of the program throughout the tenure of the demonstration.

Table 2-1. MDRC Supported Work Demonstration Sites

Location	Operating Agency
Atlanta, Georgia	PREP (Preparation for Employment Program), a unit of the Atlanta Urban League
Chicago, Illinois	Options, Inc., a nonprofit agency set up to operate supported work
Detroit, Michigan	Supported Work Corporation, a nonprofit agency set up to operate supported work
Hartford, Connecticut	The Maverick Corporation, a nonprofit agency set up to operate supported work
Jersey City, New Jersey	Community Help Corporation, a nonprofit agency set up to operate supported work
Massachusetts	Transitional Employment Enterprises, a nonprofit agency set up to operate supported work
Newark, New Jersey	Newark Service Corporation, a nonprofit agency set up to operate supported work
New York, New York	Wildcat Service Corporation, a nonprofit agency established by the Vera Institute of Justice to operate supported work
Oakland, California (Alameda County)	Peralta Service Corporation, a nonprofit agency established by the Spanish Speaking Unity Council to operate supported work
Philadelphia, Pennsylvania	Impact Service Corporation, a nonprofit agency set up to operate supported work
St. Louis, Missouri	A unit of the St. Louis Housing Authority
San Francisco, California	The San Francisco Phoenix Corporation, a nonprofit agency set up to operate supported work
Washington State	Pivot, a nonprofit agency set up to operate supported work
West Virginia (Five counties in the northwest area of the state)	A unit of the Human Resource Development Foundation, Inc., a subsidiary of the West Virginia Labor Federation, AFL-CIO
Wisconsin (Fond du Lac and Winnebago Counties)	A unit of Advocap, Inc., a Community Action Agency

STANDARDIZATION AND VARIABILITY

In order to assure the implementation of the supported work model and to ensure also the uniformity of program design, the requirements governing local operations established the basic features to be included in all supported work programs:

1. Detailed eligibility requirements for each of the four target groups, designed to ensure that the programs employed only the most severely disadvantaged (see Table 2-2).
2. A wage and bonus structure, established by MDRC, that accounted for differing local wage conditions (starting wage levels of the programs ranged from the then federal minimum wage of $2.30 to $3.10 per hour) but that (a) allowed bonuses and merit increases for supported workers who met gradually increasing work requirements, and (b) made sure that a participant receiving maximum supported work wages would have earnings slightly below the market opportunity wage (the average wage of entry-level jobs that the target populations could normally expect to obtain).
3. A fixed maximum term of program participation—normally 12 months, but varied to 18 months for research purposes at some sites. At that point, participants had to leave the program and, if successful, with program assistance, move on to a nonsubsidized job.
4. Implementation of the key program elements of peer support, close supervision, and graduated stress.

Table 2-2. Supported Work Eligibility Criteria, by Target Group

Target Group	Eligibility Criteria[a]
AFDC	Women on AFDC both currently and for 30 out of the preceding 36 months; youngest child 6 years old or older
Ex-addicts	Age 18 years or older; enrolled in a drug treatment program currently or within the preceding 6 months
Ex-offenders	Age 18 years or older; incarcerated within the last 6 months as a result of a conviction
Youths	Age 17 to 20 years; no high school or equivalency degree; not in school in the last 6 months; delinquency record, conviction, court appearance, or similar (for at least 50% of the youth)
All groups	Currently unemployed[b]; spent no more than 3 months in a job during the past 6 months

[a]Supported work eligibility criteria refer to conditions prevailing at the time of application to the supported work program. If a person in supported work voluntarily or involuntarily leaves the program and subsequently reapplies for a supported work job, he or she is not reviewed again for acceptance under the eligibility criteria.

[b]Worked no more than 10 hours a week for the last 4 weeks.

The key program elements were implemented by different techniques, but each had to be approved by MDRC. For example, peer support was made possible by developing worksites manned by crews, usually between four and ten workers. Some programs featured regular crew meetings to discuss the worksite problems and air grievances; several introduced a formal management-by-objectives planning and productivity review process for each work crew. Many designated crew chiefs, choosing for this management role participants who were performing well above minimum requirements.

The local programs implemented the graduated stress concept in various ways: by increasing productivity demands and attendance and punctuality requirements; by assigning workers to increasingly complex work assignments; or by gradually decreasing the degree of supervision.

Effective supervision was implemented in most cases by assigning a program supervisor to 8 to 12 participants, and having that supervisor evaluate each worker's performance frequently and communicate the assessment to the participant.

Supported work guidelines did not allow the use of ancillary services, such as personal counseling, on paid time, but did permit 25 percent of paid time to be used for support services that MDRC guidelines defined as "work-related." These included orientation, skill training, and job readiness and placement activities. But generally, local programs made only limited use of this feature, using about 6 percent of paid time for allowable support services. The rest was work.

The other key aspects of local operation, such as the kind of local organization operating the program and the type of worksite, were allowed to vary. However, MDRC monitored these aspects closely, and all proposed variations required approval. What resulted was a wide range of activities. Nearly 900,000 participant days of work were spent in six major industrial areas. As Table 2-3 indicates, over one-half of work time was spent in service activities, ranging from building maintenance and security to day care; one-quarter of the time was devoted to construction work; and almost 10 percent was in manufacturing. There was a great deal of diversity among the various sites in areas of concentration. Male and female participants worked in all these jobs, with female participants more heavily represented in the service activities. Work was done for a broad range of customers, including private individuals (11 percent), and organizations in the profit (11 percent), non-profit (32 percent), and public (46 percent) sectors.

Local programs sought to develop and maintain variety in their

Table 2-3. Percentage Distribution of Project Days in Major Industries in the 15 Supported Work Programs by Site, during the Period March 1975 through December 1978

Major Industries	Atlanta	Chicago	Detroit	Hartford	Jersey City	Massachusetts	New York	Newark	Oakland	Philadelphia	St. Louis	San Francisco	Washington	West Virginia	Wisconsin	All Sites
Agriculture[a]	.2		4.7	2.7			.3	1.3	21.1	15.6		6.1	1.0	5.2	.6	3.5
Construction																
Resid. Bldg. Rehab.	1.1	1.7	3.1	19.4	9.6	2.6						.6				6.2
Non-res. Bldg. Rehab.	1.4		23.5	.2	15.3	14.1	.7	3.8		3.2		3.2	3.0	.9	31.1	3.6
Painting	10.2	18.9	4.7	6.1	3.3	.7	.6	1.5	30.7	7.0	6.3	13.7	.3	2.0	.7	6.8
Deleading		1.5			2.4	38.8		1.7	4.0	6.2				2.1		3.5
Other	2.0	13.3	31.6	.1	8.1	1.6	1.0	.4	3.0	43.5		20.1	15.6	11.5	7.9	8.2
Total	14.7	35.4	62.9	25.8	38.7	57.8	2.3	7.3	37.7	59.9	6.3	37.7	18.9	16.4	40.7	28.3
Manufacturing	7.9	10.3	.9	20.4	5.1	17.4		8.3	3.8	.7			33.1	2.5	.9	7.8
Transportation, Communication	13.8			4.2	12.3		.1	.2	6.7		2.9	6.1		6.2	1.4	4.5
Wholesale, Retail Trade[b]	.7		.1	3.4	12.0	1.3	.9	3.4	11.9	1.4	21.4	5.1	.3		1.1	4.2
Services																
Clerical	15.5	15.9	5.3	3.0	5.2	.7	12.3	10.5	6.4	4.6	8.5	8.7	3.9	7.1	6.7	7.9
Building Maint.	17.1	.4	9.7	3.1	15.9	2.8	7.5	22.8	3.3	3.6		10.8	5.0	17.6	21.7	10.0
Other Business	.9	20.6	7.6	.2	6.6	11.0	62.1	31.7	8.4	5.6	8.3	10.4	32.9	10.7	8.7	16.8
Automotive	17.2			7.5	1.7	.3		1.2		3.5			1.6	3.7	1.4	2.7
Misc. Repair				29.7				.5	.5				3.2	5.8	15.9	4.7
Health	13.0										15.1			3.1		1.7
Education	9.7	3.4	2.5		2.3		.2	2.1			10.2			5.2	.2	1.5
Social	3.5		6.2				14.2	10.5			25.7	15.2		13.7	.7	5.4
Other					.1	8.6		.3		5.0	1.6			2.2		1.1
Total	76.7	40.3	31.3	43.5	31.9	23.4	96.3	79.6	18.8	22.4	69.4	45.1	46.9	69.4	55.2	51.7
Total	100.0	100.0	100.0	100.0	100.0	100.0	100.0	100.0	100.0	100.0	100.0	100.0	100.0	100.0	100.0	100.0
Total Project Days	45,099	79,178	17,990	91,706	111,447	49,140	80,888	87,827	61,843	47,261	28,684	21,978	34,147	54,440	49,529	861,157

Source: Tabulations of time sheet and project data in the Supported Work Management Information System.

Notes: Industry categories were taken from the Standard Industrial Classification (SIC) system of the U.S. Department of Labor, Office of Management and Budget. Although this system is structured to classify establishments under various categories, the supported work demonstration has adapted the definitions to apply to the work being performed. The information is provided by site on MIS project description forms.

Project days were calculated by dividing project hours by 8, for all sites except Wisconsin, where the number of hours worked per day is 7.5.

Detailed percentage distributions may not add exactly to total because of rounding.

Percentages within industry have been proportionately adjusted to compensate for a small number of project days for which industry classification could not be determined at the time of the analysis.

[a] Includes landscaping work.
[b] Includes food service.

worksites. Some worksites offered simple tasks with minimum stress, whereas others were more complex; some were public service jobs, and others were revenue producing. Worksites were generally composed of crews of more than one target group, and the research results show no indication that any one configuration of target populations or any particular type of work resulted in better in-program performance.

Some worksites were more demanding and creative than those normally found in manpower programs. Over the course of the demonstration, individual programs did such varied things as fabricate molded concrete products; operate a restaurant; construct small boats; manage a public park and golf course; build and operate a child care center; and rehabilitate, with some new construction, a two-block inner-city area. Not all these worksites survived; the restaurant and boat-building operations, for example, had to be closed because of financial losses. But those that stayed in business demonstrated that supported workers could handle complex tasks and that an employment program was capable of managing these kinds of operations. The challenge to creativity required in developing these worksites and in managing them productively attracted and maintained a caliber of leadership that, in at least several cases, might not otherwise have been interested in managing a relatively small demonstration program.

Worksites were generally developed, controlled, and supervised by program operators. This meant that there was little stationing of workers outside the program. In the few cases where outstationing occurred, the worksites were unusually attractive, from a programmatic or funding perspective. The need to maintain control over the development and supervision of worksites turned the programs into miniconglomerates: a program could have from 5 to 15 different sites, each with different needs of supervision, technical expertise, production planning, quality control, work schedules, and equipment.

The programs varied in size from 100 to 300 participants. This relatively moderate scope for an employment program enabled operators to develop and manage varied, innovative, and closely supervised worksites.

Higher levels of management and technical skills were required when programs began exploring the development of revenue-generating projects. These produced goods or offered services to local agencies or businesses under contract arrangements providing for reimbursement of a portion of the worksite costs. Most programs vastly underestimated the difficulties of making money. It often took 12 to 18 months for a revenue-generating project to cover the extra expenses it incurred, particularly in cases that required capital investment. MDRC provided assistance in the planning, financial forecasting, production, and marketing operations of such worksites. By the conclusion of the demonstration, over 75 percent of all work days were partially financed by some sort of customer contract including arrangements such as: percentage of cost, cost plus fee, worker wages only, competitive bids, and retail sales. Though no program achieved financial independence, most of these revenue-generating projects were able, by the last year of the demonstration, to cover worksite expenses (supervision, equipment, supplies, etc.) and some portion of supported workers' wages with revenues.

The benefits of the development of revenue-generating worksites, though a while in coming, were considerable. They produced a wider variety of work opportunities; yielded work experience similar in type and job demands to the kinds of jobs that participants would encounter in the regular labor market; and required the program managers to plan production and focus on productivity and deadlines to a degree that nonreimbursed public service work generally does not call for. These projects probably raised worksite standards for the entire demonstration.

A key aspect of local operations was the character and style of management. The local jurisdictions selected two basic types of management to operate supported work programs. Some created new nonprofit organizations with the sole purpose of operating a supported work program. Others chose to delegate development and management of supported work projects to an existing agency with experience in operating employment programs, such as an Urban League chapter, an AFL–CIO Human Resources Development Institute affiliate, a Community Action Agency, and, in one jurisdiction, the local public housing agency. It was required, however, that existing agencies establish a separate staff unit to operate supported work. In most instances these staff units were located separately from the larger agency, and thus could focus on the specialized demands of operating supported work while still benefiting from the administrative, political, and operating experience of the larger agency.

As it turned out, supported work programs can be operated by either of these two management mechanisms. The choice depends largely on the availability of local agencies with a record that reflects potential for leadership and management. The demonstration showed that newly created, sole purpose, nonprofit organizations generally enjoyed more independence and less oversight from local authorities than units within existing agencies. The new and independent operators generated the largest programs and many of the most innovative worksites. But a price had to be paid for this risk-taking and creativity of the newly created nonprofits; they required more intensive oversight and more programmatic, administrative, and fiscal assistance from MDRC staff. The one site that MDRC closed down over the course of the demonstration was a newly formed nonprofit, with no sponsoring roof over it, and several other sites ran into serious difficulties that required extensive intervention and assistance.

Programs functioning as units within sponsoring agencies generally operated along more conventional nonprofit lines and took fewer risks than their newly established counterparts. The operating experience, knowledge of the local community, and established administrative structure of the older sponsoring agencies contributed to the development and risk avoidance of programs that operated under the guidance and with the support of the parent agencies.

All program operators had to conduct their supported work programs under the terms of an agreement negotiated annually with MDRC, and within uniform operating guidelines established by MDRC. Each annual contract set forth the program's expected performance in terms of total participants and breakdown by target group; total budget and unit cost indicators; worksites to be developed; attendance, placement, and other program performance goals—both general and specific to each site. To oversee these contracts and guidelines the MDRC staff performed frequent on-site monitoring, provided technical assistance, and participated in major staffing and operating decisions. During the demonstration, five changes in program leadership were in part attributable to MDRC intervention. This active oversight role by MDRC was designed to assure both the implementation of basic supported work principles and consistent standards for evaluating performance.

FUNDING

The initial MDRC guidelines required local operators to raise a share of the funds needed to cover operating expenses from local sources. The purpose was twofold: to use national resources as leverage for the development of a sufficiently large and viable local demonstration; and to develop a local base of support that would be the main source of funding for these programs once the national demonstration, with its large national funding commitment, had run its course. Because the national funding commitments came from a variety of federal departments (DOL, HEW, LEAA, HUD), MDRC assumed that local operators would obtain local grant funding from a variety of sources.

The local operating cost of the demonstration was $66 million (see Table 2-4), and by the end of the fourth and final year of the demonstration, the local programs were covering 58 percent of these costs from local revenues. The relatively high share of locally raised funds, however, tells only part of the local support story. The expectation that local funding sources would parallel national funding sources in their variety was not realized. Instead, most local agencies saw supported work as merely another employment program, and the local CETA agency as the appropriate local funding source. Most local supported work operators were not familiar with nonmanpower agencies and thus did not have the experience for the successful pursuit of funds from such sources. By the end of the fourth year, every supported work program had local CETA funds, with these CETA agencies contributing slightly more than 25 percent of total operating costs, or about half of all locally raised funds.

The second largest source of local revenues was the sale of goods and services produced by the program. At the end of the fourth year, the local programs covered 17 percent of their expenses with such

Table 2-4. Summary of Supported Work Demonstration Site Operations Expenditures by Funding Source and Contract Year

Sources of Funds for Site Operations[a]	Year 1	Year 2	Year 3	Year 4	Total
Income from sale of goods and services	13%	16%	16%	17%	16%
Other local funding: CETA	19	16	27	29	23
Other[b]	10	11	10	12	11
National funding (MDRC)	59	56	47	42	50
Total	100	100	100	100	100
Total site operations expenditures ($000)	8,937	19,433	23,389	14,659	66,418

Source: Tabulations of data in the Supported Work Fiscal system combined operating reports.

Notes: The data for each of the first three contract years cover totals from a 12-month period of each program's operation, with a few isolated exceptions. The Year 4 period ranged from 6 to 12 months, depending on the site. Percentage distributions may not add exactly to totals because of rounding.

[a]Includes all expenses related to the operation of the local supported work programs.

[b]Includes other forms of grants or contracts, and funds received through welfare diversion procedures.

revenues. Most sites shifted to revenue generation during the second year, when it became apparent that the expected variety of local sources would not materialize and that local CETA agencies, because of the intense competition for their allocations, would not be sufficient to provide the resources required locally for the supported work programs. This shift was, as indicated earlier, a mixed blessing. Program operators as a rule were not experienced businessmen, and it took time for them to develop the technical, marketing, and contracting expertise necessary for business-type operations. The demonstration experience shows that, because of the difficulties involved in working with these target populations, these programs can cover no more than one-third of their operating expenses out of worksite-generated revenues, and in the first years this share is likely to be much smaller.

Another critical, although smaller, component of funding was the use of welfare payments diverted to the program. MDRC obtained a federal agreement to an arrangement under which any reduction in an individual's AFDC welfare payment as a result of employment in a supported work program could be applied to cover a portion of that person's wages. These funds covered only 2 percent of the demonstration's total operating costs, but they became an important part of a local budget wherever a program employed a significant number of AFDC participants.

MDRC often acted not only as the national management and funding agency but also as banker: providing seed money to start new worksites that required capital and equipment that could not be covered locally; giving advances to assure the required cash flow when local funding reimbursements were delayed; supplying additional national funding when local funding agencies fell short of their commitments; and assisting in scaling down programs when it became clear that local funds would not be generated in sufficient amounts to meet established goals. Because supported work programs are designed to approach the style and requirements of work in the private sector, this banking, oversight, and technical assistance role of the managing agency will remain critical in any future efforts to operate supported work programs.

TARGET POPULATION AND
IN-PROGRAM PERFORMANCES

Over the period of the demonstration, March 1975–December 1978, 10,043 persons were employed as participants in the supported work programs. About 38 percent of these were ex-offenders, 21 percent AFDC recipients, 23 percent youths, and 12 percent ex-addicts. The remaining 6 percent were composed of primarily mental health outpatients and recovering alcoholics, two groups which were added to the original four in response to requests by several local program operators, but were not included in the experimental and control sample. The target groups participated in different proportions among the sites as a result of a combination of factors: the local sites' initial preferences; the relative ease or difficulty of recruitment; the availability of local funding for specific groups; and each local program's assessment of the success of each group.

The participants in the major target groups were recruited and enrolled according to eligibility criteria designed to ensure that the program was targeted to the most severely disadvantaged within these groups, but who were able to work and were not normally served by employment programs (see Table 2-2). Thus, the program focused on AFDC women who had received welfare payments for 3 years or more, had been out of the labor market for a long time, and whose children were of school age. These restrictions targeted supported work at about 15 percent of the entire AFDC population—a group that is older, less educated, has been on welfare longer, and has not worked full-time for a longer period of time than the average AFDC recipients. Ex-addicts and ex-offenders had to have been in drug treatment programs or incarcerated within the past 6 months. The youth criteria limited the program to individuals without high school diplomas, and 50 percent of the youths enrolled had to have a background of previous contact with the criminal justice system. Referrals came from a variety of sources. Over one-half were made by public agencies—federal, state, county, and local. Private, nonprofit agencies referred another 30 percent of supported work participants, and the remaining were "walk-ins," or self-referrals. The overwhelming majority of AFDC referrals at all sites were drawn from the "unassigned pool" in the WIN program.[1]

Selected characteristics of the supported work sample are presented in Tables 2-5 and 2-6.[2] The average age of the supported

---

1. The "unassigned pool" refers to all registrants who are not participating in any WIN service (such as on-the-job training, public service employment, or job search assistance) and for whom the WIN staff have not found full-time unsubsidized employment. (Specific procedures for use of the pool vary from state to state.)

2. The data in Tables 2-5 and 2-6 are for the research sample at 10 of the supported work sites. A comparison of the employment, education, and demographic characteristics of this sample with those for the 10,043 participants at the 15 sites indicates that the research sample closely matches the total participants, except that the participant sample is less heavily black and Hispanic, because the research sample did not include projects in West Virginia and Washington, where there were larger proportions of white participants.

Table 2-5. Selected Demographic Characteristics of the Supported Work Research Sample, at Enrollment, by Target Group

Characteristic	AFDC	Ex- Addicts	Ex- Offenders	Youth
Average age (years)	33.6	27.8	25.3	18.3
Percent male	0.0	80.1	94.3	86.4
Race and Ethnicity				
Percent Black, non-Hispanic	83.0	77.7	83.6	78.2
Percent Hispanic	12.1	8.2	8.8	15.6
Percent White, non-Hispanic	4.6	13.8	7.4	5.9
Percent Other	0.2	0.3	0.2	0.2
Percent currently married	3.0	23.1	11.8	3.7
Average No. dependents in household	2.2	0.9	0.4	0.2
Education				
Average years of schooling	10.3	10.6	10.4	9.7
Percent with 12 or more years	30.4	28.5	26.7	0.7
Welfare receipt month prior to enrollment[a]				
Percent with any	99.8	39.2	17.1	12.5
Average amount received ($)	284	79	29	21
Average number of years ever received welfare	8.6	—	—	—
Months since last full-time job (%)				
Now working or less than 2	3.4	11.6	7.4	12.1
2–12	11.9	31.1	20.4	37.7
13–24	9.9	20.0	22.3	19.6
25 or more	60.7	32.4	38.9	8.6
Never worked	14.2	4.9	11.0	21.9
Average weeks worked during previous 12 months	3.4	10.0	5.5	9.3
Average earnings during previous 12 months ($)	240	1,227	580	827
Number in Sample	1,351	974	1,497	861

Source: Baseline interviews administered to the research sample of individuals, experimentals and controls, at ten sites who completed the baseline, 9-month, and 18-month interviews.

Notes: Distributions may not add to 100 percent because of rounding. Data on average number of years receiving welfare are available only for the AFDC group. The data in all cases apply to the entire sample. Average numbers thus include zero values.

[a]"Welfare" includes AFDC, GA, SSI, and other unspecified cash welfare income.

Table 2-6. Selected Drug Use and Criminal History Characteristics of the Supported Work Research Sample, at Enrollment, by Target Group

Characteristic	Ex-Addicts	Ex-Offenders	Youth
Drug Use History			
Percent reporting use of heroin			
Regular use[a]	85.4	31.3	2.6
Any use	94.3	44.5	7.8
Percent reporting regular use of any drug other than marijuana[a]	88.5	36.7	4.4
Percent reporting use of marijuana	90.8	80.6	60.2
Percent in drug treatment last 6 months	88.6	12.2	1.7
Type of treatment			
Methadone maintenance	54.2	—	—
Drug-free program	21.3	—	—
Other type of treatment	24.5	—	—
Criminal History			
Arrests			
Percent with any	89.6	99.6	54.2
Average number	8.3	9.2	2.2
Convictions			
Percent with any	74.7	95.0	34.0
Average number	2.9	3.0	0.6
Average number of weeks ever incarcerated	129	195	20
Percent ever incarcerated	69.6	96.0	27.9
Number in Sample	974	1,497	861

Source: Baseline interviews administered to the research sample of individuals, experimentals and controls, who completed baseline, 9-month, and 18-month interviews.

Notes: Questions pertaining to drug use or criminal histories were not administered to the AFDC population. Similarly, data on type of drug treatment are not available for other than the ex-addict group.

Eligibility requirements for participation in the demonstration specify a history of drug use for ex-addicts and of incarceration for ex-offenders. However, the sample of ex-addicts reports less than 100 percent drug use, and the sample of ex-offenders less than 100 percent incarceration. This could reflect either that the ineligibility of certain respondents was not detected by program operators, or that the respondents have inaccurately reported their histories in these areas during the research interviews. The data in all cases apply to the entire sample. Average numbers thus include zero values.

[a]"Regular" use refers to those individuals who reported drug use at least once a day for at least two months.

workers ranges from 18 years for the youths to 34 years for the AFDC women. Over 80 percent of the individuals in every group were black or Hispanic and, excluding the AFDC women, 80 percent or more were male. The average person completed 10 years of school, and less than one-third had completed 12 years of education or more. Supported workers had limited prior employment experience, particularly in the AFDC group, 75 percent of whom had either never worked before, or had not worked for at least two years. Average earnings during the previous 12 months were equally unimpressive, ranging from $240 to $1,227 across the target groups. By definition, all of the AFDC women received welfare in the month prior to enrollment, and this group averaged a total of 8.6 years on welfare. For the other three groups, those on welfare ranged from 12 percent to 39 percent.

The ex-offenders and ex-addicts had extensive records of arrests and convictions, averaging eight to nine arrests and three convictions. The totals were lower but still important for the youths, who averaged two arrests and close to one conviction. Ex-addicts naturally had high drug use, with 94 percent reporting heroin use. Heroin use also was substantial, 45 percent among the ex-offenders. Among the youths, 8 percent reported prior heroin use.

The participants were thus poor, minimally educated, with little connection to and experience with the regular labor market but with considerable links to and experience with criminal justice and public assistance agencies.

A comparison of the characteristics of supported workers with those of individuals working in CETA jobs and enrolled in the Work Incentive (WIN) Program suggests that supported work served a more disadvantaged group than on average participated in these other programs. For example, compared to participants in the public service components of CETA Titles I, II, and VI, supported workers are much more likely to be black or Hispanic, have less education, are more dependent on public assistance, and have less prior work experience.[3]

These differences in the characteristics of the groups were the result of the deliberate supported work policy of serving the most disadvantaged groups. As CETA, under its new legislation, begins to

3. Comparative data for fiscal year 1976 are reported in the *Second Annual Report on the National Supported Work Demonstration*, Manpower Demonstration Research Corporation, April 1978. A subsequent unpublished analysis of CETA data for fiscal years 1977 and 1978 indicates that the large differences between CETA and supported work enrollees continued into these later years.

target more of its resources to the severely disadvantaged, it may find the lessons of supported work of some value.

With few exceptions the various local programs had little difficulty in reaching and recruiting the eligible populations. Because supported work wages are close to the minimum and because there is no guarantee of a job at the end of the 12- or 18-month demonstration, one could expect difficulty in attracting people to the program. Yet they enrolled quite readily. In addition, their performance while in the program indicates that a substantial number are not only motivated to take a job, but with the appropriate support and supervision, can hold it (see Table 2-7).

The program achieved an overall attendance rate of 83 percent for all target groups; the AFDC group achieved the highest rate (89.8 percent). Youths ranked the lowest at 75.8 percent; most local operators report that the 5-day, 40-hour work week imposed by the supported work model may be too inflexible to deal with the youth population.

Supported workers stayed an average of 6.7 months in the program, but there was substantial variation among the target groups. AFDC participants remained longest (9.5 months), and ex-offenders the most briefly (5.2 months), suggesting that the AFDC participants found the program more rewarding and were better able to adjust to the work routine. This is also reflected in the statistics on program terminations. Of all supported workers, 30 percent were fired for poor performance, but again there are large differences among target groups: only 11 percent of the AFDC group had to be terminated for performance reasons, compared to 37 percent of the ex-addicts and youths.

Almost 30 percent of all participants moved on to full-time jobs upon leaving supported work. The AFDC group was most successful in finding regular jobs (35 percent). Moreover, the steady increase in the average demonstration-wide placement rate—from 23.6 percent in the first year to 36.1 percent in the fourth—indicates that it takes time to acquire the special skills required for successful job development and placement of the severely disadvantaged. The final supported work transition rates, when compared to those in CETA Titles II and VI programs, are quite similar, even though each is serving a somewhat different population.

Table 2-7 also indicates that a substantial share (25 percent) of the AFDC terminations were mandatory. These were participants who had reached the maximum stay in the program and who had not yet been placed in a job—indicating that the programs had

Table 2-7. Summary of Key Operational Performance Indicators from the 15 Supported Work Programs during the Period March 1975 through December 1978, by Target Group

Performance Indicators	AFDC	Ex-Addicts	Ex-Offenders	Youth	Other[a]	Total
Attendance rate (%)	89.8	83.9	80.3	75.8	85.6	83.0
Average length of participation, in months	9.5	6.8	5.2	6.8	7.6	6.7
Distribution of departures by type (%)						
Firings	10.9	37.3	32.5	37.2	26.0	29.7
Other negative terminations	7.5	14.6	20.0	16.1	7.6	15.4
Mandatory graduation	24.8	10.7	4.1	5.3	7.7	9.3
Other neutral terminations	20.8	12.3	12.2	12.6	18.6	14.0
Terminations to school	1.5	1.9	2.3	3.0	6.2	2.5
Terminations to a job	34.6	23.1	28.9	25.8	33.9	28.9
Average hourly placement wage ($)	3.43	3.97	4.02	3.20	3.26	3.63
Average public subsidy cost per person ($)b	8,139	5,825	4,455	5,826	6,511	5,740
Average public subsidy cost per service-year ($)b			10,281			

Source: Tabulations of status activity and timesheet data in the Supported Work Management Information System and of data from the Supported Work fiscal system combined operating reports.

Notes: Attendance rates were calculated by dividing total attendance time by the total participant days minus scheduled absence days (holidays and vacation) and inactivations (leaves of absence). "Other Negative" departures include incarcerations, reinstitutionalizations, and resignations because of dissatisfaction with the supported work job. "Mandatory Graduations," are departures that occur when supported workers reach the maximum allowable length of stay in the program without having found post-program employment. "Other Neutral" departures include such things as death and resignations for reasons of personal or family health problems. Percentage distributions may not add exactly to 100 because of rounding.

aThe "other" target group is composed primarily of ex-alcoholics (Jersey City and Massachusetts) and mentally disabled employees (Wisconsin).

bBased on the average public subsidy costs during the third and fourth years of the demonstration.

difficulty in developing acceptable regular labor market jobs for even this relatively successful group of employees.

Finally, the average public cost (total expenditures minus worksite revenues) of providing a participant with one year of supported work employment was about $13,000 during the first year of the demonstration and declined to $10,281 by the third and fourth years of operations (see Table 2-8). This decline in costs, despite increases in the minimum wage and general inflation, can be attributed to several factors: the relatively high start-up costs during the first year, and an increase in scale and greater operating efficiency over the later years of the demonstration. Because the average supported worker spent only 6.7 months in the program, the $10,281 figure translates into a per-person cost of $5,740 for all target groups, ranging from $4,455 per ex-offender participant to $8,139 per AFDC participant, depending on average stay in the program. Of this public subsidy, 57 percent went directly to participants in the form of wages and fringe benefits, with the rest covering overhead, supervision, materials, and supplies.

As Table 2-8 indicates, per year of service, employment in supported work is more costly than CETA public service employment and close in cost to the Job Corps. However, the difference in supported work and CETA costs may in large part reflect variations in accounting practices: supported work costs include all expenditures for overhead, supervision, and materials, which in CETA-PSE

Table 2-8. Comparison of the Public Subsidy Cost of Supported Work with the Average Cost for Selected Employment Programs

Program	Average Cost per Service Year	Average Length of Stay in Months	Average Cost per Participant[a]
Supported work	$10,281	6.7	$5,740
Job Corps	10,253	5.6	4,785
CETA Titles II, VI Public service employment	8,785	11.3	8,273

Sources: Supported Work data: tabulations of data in the Supported Work fiscal system combined operating reports and the Management Information System. Average cost per service year is based on the average public subsidy costs during the third and fourth years of the demonstration. Job Corps data: *Job Corps in Brief, FY-78*, U.S. Department of Labor, Employment and Training Administration. CETA data: *Analysis of Titles I, II, and VI of the Comprehensive Employment and Training Act of 1973 for Fiscal Year 1978*, Office of Community Employment Programs, U.S. Department of Labor, May 1979.

[a]Average cost per participant was computed by applying the average length of stay to the average cost per service year.

are usually incurred by the sponsoring agencies and which are not accounted for in reported program costs. Moreover, as Table 2–8 also shows, on a per-person basis, supported work costs compare favorably to CETA and are only slightly above those of the Job Corps, reflecting the different lengths of time that people stay in the three programs.

Thus, data from the 15 demonstration sites suggest that it costs slightly more to employ the severely disadvantaged target groups enrolled in supported work, and that it is somewhat more difficult for them to move into regular employment, than is the case for the participants in other employment programs. This indicates that a highly structured program, specially designed for those who do not generally participate in CETA and WIN programs, can be operated with a relatively minor increase in public funds, and can place these hard-to-employ groups in regular jobs at almost the rate that less specialized programs achieve for their participants.

However, all these data are the product of the period during which participants were enrolled in the program. They do not speak to the record of supported work in reaching its long-term objective of affecting the work performance and behavior of supported workers in regular jobs and in their communities. Subsequent chapters will examine these results and their cost.

✳ *Chapter 3*

The Supported Work Research Design

From the very outset, the funders and planners of the national supported work demonstration were committed to securing useful, accurate data from their undertaking. All agreed that this was essential to avoid the deficiencies of many previous evaluations of employment programs, which had been criticized for their failure to produce reliable and policy-relevant findings. Objections had been raised to several procedures employed in these earlier studies including: that inappropriate comparison groups had been used in the evaluation of the performance of the program participants; that there was not comprehensive cost accounting; and that data were gathered from small samples, drawn from single (perhaps atypical, "hot house") projects, or collected over an insufficient follow-up period. Within the budgetary and time limitations and the operating constraints, the research on the supported work demonstration attempted to steer clear of these shortcomings.

Early in the planning process, the Manpower Demonstration Research Corporation (MDRC) Board and the funders defined the following basic research questions.

1. How effective is supported work in increasing the long-term employment and earnings of participants and in reducing welfare dependency, criminal activities, or drug abuse?
2. What target populations benefit most from the program?
3. What does the program cost? To what extent does it produce

valuable goods and services? How do the program's costs compare to its measurable benefits?
4. What local conditions, administrative auspices, and implementation strategies seem to be most conducive to success?
5. What characteristics of the program model have the greatest impact on participant performance and behavior?

These questions reflect the interests of the funding agencies and the Board, and the perceptions of the Board and the researchers as to what could be feasibly answered given the amount of money available for the demonstration. It was recognized that all aspects of the questions could not be examined, but the results reflect an effort to provide definitive answers to some parts of the agenda.

The plan to answer these questions fell logically into three relatively separate components: the behavioral (impact) analysis, the benefit-cost analysis, and the process/documentation analysis. MDRC had overall responsibility for the design and management of all aspects of the research. The evaluation of program impact and cost and the statistical process analysis were conducted by researchers at Mathematica Policy Research and the Institute for Research on Poverty of the University of Wisconsin. The documentation analysis was the direct responsibility of MDRC staff and consultants.

The behavioral analysis addressed the issues raised in questions 1 and 2. It attempted to quantify the short- and longer term effects of supported work on the employment and income, welfare receipt, criminal activities, and drug abuse of participants. The strategy used to investigate these effects, the principal topic of this chapter, is discussed below. The results of this analysis are summarized in Chapters 4–7 and presented in full in a forthcoming series of final reports on the individual target groups.

The benefit-cost analysis dealt with the subsections of question 3. It endeavored to estimate, in economic terms, the net benefits (or costs) of supported work. These benefits and costs were considered from three perspectives: that of society in general, that of those who were offered a supported work job, and that of the remainder of society. This analysis drew, in large part, upon the conclusions of the behavioral analysis, because the benefits of the program were expected to include increases in the economic status of the participants and reductions in their dependence on welfare, crime, and drugs. A second major data source was the uniform comprehensive fiscal and management information system that registered data at all sites. It provided detailed and complete information on overhead costs; on the resources and manpower used in individual work projects; and on the behavior of program participants (e.g., their average stay in the program or other operational indices reported in Chapter 2). Finally, because supported work was an employment program, another principal source of benefits and costs was the value of the work performed by program participants and the associated cost of tools, project supervision, raw materials, and inventory. These were estimated for a sample of 44 work projects at various program sites based on detailed calculations of the prices of both inputs and outputs. A more detailed discussion of the benefit-cost methodology can be found in Chapter 8, where a summary of the results from the analysis is reported.

Finally, in an effort to answer questions 4 and 5, a multifaceted process/documentation analysis was attempted. The objective was to determine what operational characteristics were correlated with performance. The analysis involved a statistical effort to discover the interrelationships among the various program elements and the in- and post-program performance of participants, as well as a more qualitative attempt to account for local variations in the quality of leadership; in the types of job creation, placement, and funding strategies; and in the geographic, economic, and political environments. The statistical effort was both innovative and exploratory, and sought to use the extensive and detailed program information recorded in the supported work management information system in combination with the interview data to develop rigorous measures of the effectiveness of alternative program treatments. In general, this effort was not very successful and contributed little to an understanding of the usefulness of the components of supported work. The more qualitative assessment relied primarily on the observations of MDRC's research and operations staffs and on the reports of consultants. The results of these analyses are not discussed in detail in this report, though they have informed the discussion in Chapter 2 and recommendations of the Board of Directors. Many of the studies are available as separate MDRC publications, including reports on worksite development, job placement procedures, and local demonstration funding.

The behavioral (impact) analysis was the heart of the research endeavor. Important in its own right, it also provided information vital to the benefit-cost and statistical process analyses.

THE BEHAVIORAL ANALYSIS

Research Hypotheses

The primary task of the evaluation was to determine whether supported work participation resulted in changes in the employment and other behavior of the members of the four target groups. For each and all target groups, the research was to test the hypothesis that participants would have more stable, long-term post-supported work employment experiences and higher long-term earnings, and that they would be less dependent on transfer payments such as AFDC, general assistance, and Medicaid. In addition, the research was to test hypotheses related to ex-addicts and ex-offenders: would supported work reduce the likelihood of reversion to drug use or criminal activities, and if offenses were committed, would they be less serious? For the youth group, it was hypothesized that supported work would reduce the criminal activities of the delinquent subpopulation and increase the likelihood of return-to-school among the entire population. Finally, for all target groups, the evaluation tested a number of questions concerning the effects of supported work on housing consumption and public housing tenancy.

Research Methodology

Random Assignment.   To determine the effect of supported work on those who participate, it is necessary to have a measure of what the participant group would have done in the absence of the program. In the most convincing previous evaluations of large-scale manpower programs, this was done by establishing a comparison group of nonparticipating individuals similar to those who joined the program. Data on the program participants and members of the comparison group could then be examined, and differences between both the groups ascribed to the program.

Prior to the national supported work demonstration, no large-scale employment program had used the most reliable means of ensuring identical participant and comparison groups—random assignment—and there was substantial concern that such a procedure would be adamantly opposed by program operators. In designing the demonstration, however, it was decided that the benefits of this procedure outweighed the risks, and a random procedure was adopted. It assigned individuals to either the experimental group (offered a supported work job) or the control group (excluded from supported work). The use of this procedure allowed the researchers to attribute, with well-established degrees of statistical confidence, any experiment-control differences to the effects of the program, rather than to unmeasured differences between the two groups.

There was initial resistance to random assignment by some referral agencies and program operators, who felt the process was unfair to controls and necessitated too large a recruiting effort. As the demonstration progressed, however, operators became more familiar with the process, complaints diminished and eventually disappeared, and the procedure became only a minor operational annoyance. During the 2.5 years when random assignment was in operation (March 1975–July 1977), over 6,600 applicants were subjected to the process.[1] Assignments were made by computer under the control of centrally located Mathematica personnel. After assignment (see Figure 3–1), both groups were given a baseline interview to determine their prior employment, welfare, criminal activities, and drug-use histories. At two of the sites, interviews were given before random assignment to see if the procedure itself affected the respondents' survey answers; statistical analysis showed that it did not do so.

In addition to the baseline interview, members of the sample were periodically reinterviewed by Mathematica survey staff to determine their subsequent activities, and were paid either $5 or $10 per interview. Finally, to preserve the integrity of the research design, the experimental group included all individuals randomly assigned to a supported work job, even those who did not appear for their first day of work or who quit soon thereafter. (Whereas only 3 percent of the experimentals never worked in the program, a substantial number, about 25 percent, left their supported work jobs within the first 3 months.)

Sample Size, Follow-up, and Site Distribution. In an effort to avoid the weakness of earlier evaluations, the designers of the supported work demonstration sought a sample sufficiently large to provide a good prospect of detecting program effects at statistically significant levels. They also provided for a follow-up period sufficiently long to permit the discovery of post-program effects. And they wanted the sample to come from an adequate number of the program sites to assure that the findings would be representative of the variety of operating styles and local conditions that need to be accommodated in a national program.

In their effort to meet these objectives within the project's fixed

1. The random assignment of program *applicants*, rather than a sample of *typical program eligibles* who might or might not want to participate, was adopted as a means to reduce research costs. The initial design had called for random assignment of roughly 20,000 individuals on file at the various referral agencies. Even though the design would have provided additional information on the size and nature of the potential pool of program enrollees and on their likely interest in the program, it would have cost three times as much as the selected design.

Figure 3-1

INTAKE PROCESS IN THE SUPPORTED WORK DEMONSTRATION IN SITES WITH RANDOM ASSIGNMENT

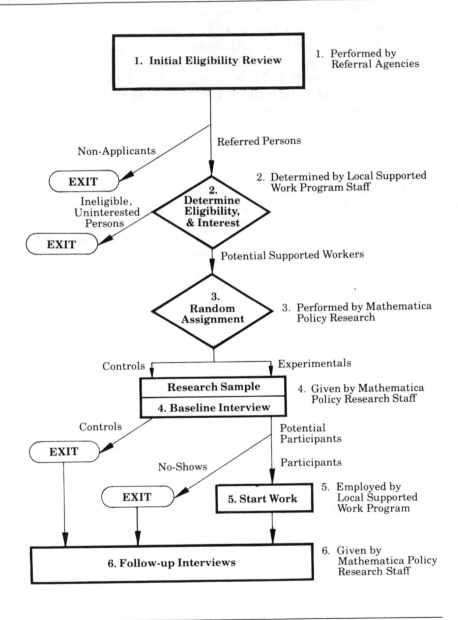

research budget and 5-year timetable, MDRC staff and Mathematica and Wisconsin researchers had to consider both actual operational conditions at the local supported work sites and the cost and yield of different parameters of the survey. Developments at the local sites were important both because there had to be a supported work job slot before any experimental could be added to the sample, and because the cost of an interview depended on the volume of interviews conducted. Thus, it was important to conduct random assignment in sites with reasonably large programs enrolling the needed target groups and during periods of rapid build-up. Survey costs depended on the size of the sample, on the number of sites with random assignment, on the time spent conducting follow-up interviews, and on certain unknown factors such as the difficulty that the interviewers would have locating the sample at different points in time after the baseline interview. Because costs could not be accurately determined at the outset, the experimental design was not set rigidly at the beginning of the project. Instead, a flexible approach was adopted that allowed research managers to track closely key factors affecting the survey budget and sample yield, and to readjust the sample allocation across sites and time periods in response to changes in these factors.

The result of this procedure was an experimental design with several unusual features, some of which proved useful while others created difficulties.

1. Sites with Random Assignment Ten demonstration sites were selected for the implementation of random assignment. Beginning in April 1975 at the first site and in mid-1976 at the last, all supported workers were hired under this procedure until it was terminated in July 1977. The staggered start-up of random assignment reflected an effort both to control costs—by delaying the start-up of the survey at a site until the volume of intake was substantial—and to avoid concentrating the research on participants enrolling in the program during its first year, which was likely to be atypical. Thus, random assignment continued over a total of almost 2.5 years, yielding a research sample made up of individuals whose total supported work experience spanned the entire period of the demonstration.

A somewhat different time frame was used for the AFDC sample, for whom the start of random assignment was postponed until early 1976 because of delays in obtaining waivers to the Social Security Act necessary for funding and general operations. The resulting threatened shortfall in the AFDC sample prompted MDRC to add a major new demonstration city (New York) and to request that 4 of the original 13 sites add AFDC participants. As a result, the AFDC and ex-offender samples were drawn from 7 sites, the youth sample from 5, and the ex-addict sample from 4 sites (see Table 3-1).

   2. Sample Size by Length of Follow-Up   In an effort to maximize the size of the overall sample and the length of its follow-up within the time frame of the demonstration, a procedure was adopted whereby all members of the sample were not followed for the same length of time. Although everyone was scheduled to have a baseline interview and the first and second follow-up interviews (at 9 and 18 months after their enrollment in the sample), only the early enrollees were interviewed at 27 and 36 months after enrollment. Given the relationship between cost per interview and the volume of interviews, this procedure produced the most interviews at the least cost, for all survey field offices at the 10 sites gave all possible follow-up interviews while they were in operation, and then closed down simultaneously on March 30, 1979. As a result, any sample member who was enrolled after March 30, 1976 did not receive a 36-month interview, and any member who was enrolled after December 31, 1976 did not receive a 27-month interview. Moreover, because of their delayed enrollment in the sample, none of the AFDC group was followed for more than 27 months. (To remedy this situation, an additional round of AFDC interviews was conducted in the fall of 1979 and will be analyzed in a supplemental report to be issued in mid-1980.)
   Table 3-1 summarizes the sample that resulted from this strategy. A total of 6,500 people had baseline interviews: 1,597 AFDC women, 1,394 ex-addicts, 2,268 ex-offenders, and 1,241 youth. All of these individuals were scheduled for 9- and 18-month interviews, although because of the anticipated problems in locating people, the actual completed interviews were lower, ranging from 73 percent to 89 percent of the assigned interviews for the 9-month interview and 67 to 84 percent for the 18-month interview. Depending on the target group, 48 to 85 percent of the research sample were assigned 27-month interviews and 16 to 33 percent 36-month interviews. A total of 3,006 27-month interviews and 774 36-month interviews were conducted. Overall, completion rates for the last two interviews ranged from 60 to 79 percent of those actually assigned. Finally, because interviewing began at different dates in the 10 sites, the 36-month sample was concentrated in a small number of the early sites, notably Jersey City and Philadelphia (see Table 3-1).

Table 3-1. Key Features of the Experimental Design and Its Implementation

Design Feature	Criteria or Outcome
Initial sample and control group strategy	Random assignment of 6,616 eligible program applicants to participant (3,214) and control (3,402) groups.
Data collection strategy	In-person interviews conducted at time of random assignment and 9-month intervals thereafter for up to 36 months. Data validated by comparison with Social Security, welfare, and arrest records.
Sites with random assignment	AFDC: Atlanta, Chicago, Hartford, Newark, New York, Oakland, Wisconsin Ex-addicts: Chicago,[a] Jersey City,[a] Oakland, Philadelphia[a] Ex-offenders: Chicago,[a] Hartford, Jersey City,[a] Newark, Oakland, Philadelphia,[a] San Francisco[a] Youth: Atlanta, Hartford, Jersey City,[a] New York, Philadelphia[a]

Final number of completed interviews and completion rates,[b] by length of follow-up

	AFDC	Ex-Addicts	Ex-Offenders	Youth
Baseline	1,597 (98.6)	1,394 (97.3)	2,268 (98.4)	1,241 (99.1)
9-month	1,440 (88.9)	1,111 (77.5)	1,682 (72.8)	1,001 (80.0)
18-month	1,362 (84.1)	987 (68.9)	1,539 (66.6)	924 (73.8)
27-month	620 (79.2)	885 (72.5)	995 (62.9)	506 (70.4)
36-month	0[c]	317 (67.2)	302 (59.8)	155 (76.7)

Percent of baseline sample assigned each type of follow-up interview

	AFDC	Ex-Addicts	Ex-Offenders	Youth
9-, 18-mo.	100	100	100	100
27-month	48.3	85.1	68.5	57.4
36-month	0[c]	32.9	21.9	16.1

Continuous cohorts: size of samples with continuous follow-up information by length of longest follow-up

	AFDC	Ex-Addicts	Ex-Offenders	Youth
18 mo.	764	225	636	436
27 mo.	587	495	609	298
36 mo.	0[c]	242	219	121

[a]Sites with 40 or more 36-month interviews.

[b]Completion rates (shown in parentheses) are calculated as a percent of the number of assigned interviews.

[c]No 36-month interviews were scheduled for the AFDC sample as a result of a delay in program start-up for this group.

3. The Cohort Phenomenon   Although the follow-up strategy adopted in the demonstration provided the largest affordable sample, it resulted in a complication referred to frequently in Chapters 4 through 8 as the cohort phenomenon. In this procedure, individuals in the sample belong to cohorts or subgroups with different lengths of follow-up depending on when they entered supported work. Because of the way it was selected, the sample with the longest follow-up may not be typical of the full research sample: these individuals were enrolled in 1975 and 1976, in periods of particularly high rates of unemployment; were concentrated in certain sites; and participated in the program during the first year or two of operations, when supported work may have been either atypically weak or particularly dynamic.

Because the goal of the research effort is to determine the effectiveness of the full demonstration—and not just of some sites with early enrollees—it is important to determine the extent to which the experiences of the early sample parallel those of the later enrollees. To the extent that they differ, the differences might provide insights on the performance of supported work under diverse local or operational conditions. Such information might help in determining the likely impact of a future program operating in a changed environment.

This cohort phenomenon is handled in different ways in the following chapters. In Chapters 4 through 8, the presentation of interview findings on each target group combines the data from the different cohorts, as indicated in the middle panel of Table 3-1, to show the program's impact on the full sample over time. Where cohort differences seem important, data on the smaller distinct samples with continuous and different lengths of follow-up—the bottom panel in Table 3-1—are presented. In the discussion of the benefits and costs in Chapter 7, alternative estimates of long-term impacts are developed, using several sets of assumptions about which cohort's behavior is more typical. In addition, a benchmark, or best guess estimate, averages the behavior of the 27- and 36-month cohorts. It is hoped that this approach has yielded a more balanced, conservative estimate of the program's overall net benefits than would have followed from a reliance solely on the small 36-month cohort.

Data Reliability.   In addition to the standard survey validation techniques, a considerable effort was made to verify the information collected in the supported work survey. Sophisticated statistical tests were applied to the results to check for any bias because of differential rates of response to the interviews. (The tests indicated that the findings were substantially free from response bias.) Similarly, in an effort to check upon the survey responses to questions concerning income, welfare receipt, and criminal activities, selected official records were consulted. Social Security records, welfare department files, and police arrest records for samples of surveyed individuals were compared to the interview responses. Some underreporting of income and arrests was uncovered, but it was largely unbiased between experimentals and controls and not of a magnitude sufficient to alter the conclusions drawn from the survey and reported in Chapters 4 through 8 below.

✳ *Chapter 4*

Findings for the AFDC Target Group

This chapter summarizes the findings of supported work's impact on the AFDC target group by comparing the behavior of the experimentals and controls over the 27-month period covered by the interviews.[1] The discussion in Chapter 2 of the in-program performance of supported workers at the 15 demonstration sites indicated that the program was most successful with this target group. The findings from the interviews with the sample at the seven sites enrolling AFDC participants and presented in this chapter confirm this conclusion.

One of the most significant aspects of the research design of supported work is that the control group provides directly comparable information on what the experience of participants would have been, had they not joined the supported work program. It is most useful, then, to look first at the experience of the control group, which provides the context in which the supported work program was operating. In subsequent sections, these findings will be contrasted with those of the experimentals during the same period. The comparison will yield data showing the impact that the program had on the participants' performance in the labor market as well as on other aspects of their behavior.

1. The findings are presented in full in a forthcoming report by Stanley Masters and Rebecca Maynard, *The Impact of Supported Work on Long-Term Recipients of AFDC Benefits*, MDRC, 1980.

EMPLOYMENT AND INCOME
OF THE CONTROL GROUP

Figure 4–1 shows a graph of the hours worked by members of the control group from the time when these controls agreed to participate in the study through the 27-month period during which they were recurrently interviewed. It indicates two key findings. First, in spite of their interest in getting a job, evident from their application to supported work, these women on average had very little employment experience. Second, there was, despite this, a steady increase in the number of hours they worked over the 27-month period. At the beginning of the study, members of the control group were working an average of about 20 hours a month; 27 months later, this figure had risen to 45. The increase is probably the result of two facts: over the period of the supported work study, conditions in the economy and the labor market were improving (the unemployment rate fell from 7.3 percent to 5.8 percent[2]); in addition, some members of any group of unemployed individuals will, over time, find jobs, even if economic conditions do not change, because those listed as unemployed always include some who are only temporarily out of work. This phenomenon is sometimes referred to as "regression to the mean." It is estimated that of the rise in hours worked by the control group over the period of the study, an average of about 60 percent is attributable to this phenomenon of regression to the mean, and 40 percent to improving economic conditions. But even though the employment of the AFDC controls increased over time, Figure 4–2 indicates that this group continued to work substantially less than the other three target groups, which are discussed later.

Turning to welfare benefits, Figure 4–3 provides a graph of the average monthly income from these payments and from food stamps for the control group. This transfer income started at over $340 per month, and at the end of the period was around $280 per month. The decline reflects the increase in earnings, for both the food stamp program and welfare systems reduce the benefits when recipients begin to earn wages.

2. Recall that the sample was enrolled over calendar time and that not all of the sample was followed for the full 27 months. Thus, the unemployment rates cited are a weighted average of the rates at the AFDC sites for the beginning period and the ending period of the study. The average enrollment month was about January 1977, and the average date of the 27-month interview was about October 1978. Over the full 4 years of the study (March 1975 to March 1979) when individuals were enrolled and interviewed in the four target groups, the national unemployment rate declined from 8.5 to 5.7 percent.

Figure 4-1

TREND IN HOURS WORKED PER MONTH: AFDC CONTROLS

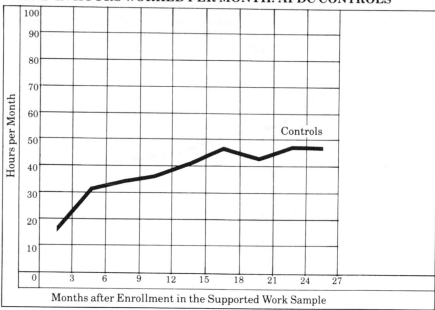

Months after Enrollment in the Supported Work Sample

Figure 4-2

TREND IN HOURS WORKED BY CONTROL GROUP MEMBERS

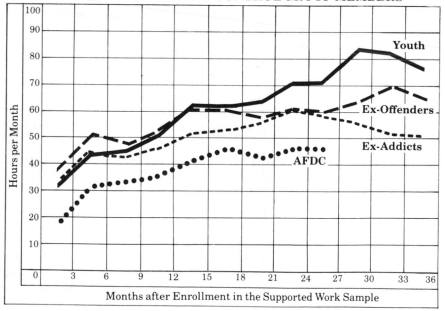

Months after Enrollment in the Supported Work Sample

Figure 4-3

TREND IN RECEIPT OF WELFARE INCOME AND FOOD STAMP BONUSES: AFDC CONTROLS

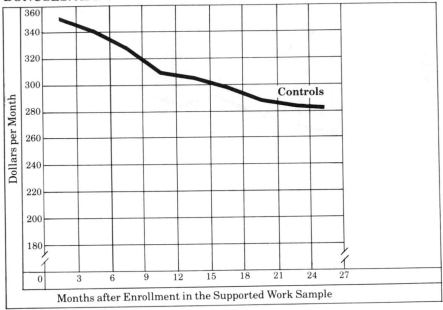

Months after Enrollment in the Supported Work Sample

Figure 4–4 shows the composition of the AFDC controls' total income in the three 9-month periods of analysis: the first 9 months after enrollment in the study; months 10 to 18; and months 19 to 27. The chart shows that, as earnings increased as a proportion of total income, payments from welfare and food stamps decreased. Overall, from the first 9 months to the last 9 months, earnings by the members of the control group increased by about $87 per month. The income of this group over the same period increased by $35. Thus, the increase in total income was much less than the income from wages: the reduction of welfare and food stamp assistance reduced the net addition to their income by 60 percent of the actual wage earned. These figures point up a problem that has been a concern of policy analysts for the last decade: how to provide work incentives to key groups of the welfare population. The fact that benefits decrease as earnings increase is bound to reduce the incentives of members of this population to seek employment. But it is not a simple quid pro quo, for though the AFDC control group in the study faced these disincentives, they still increased the number of hours they worked.

Figure 4-4

COMPONENTS OF AVERAGE TOTAL MONTHLY INCOME BY 9 MONTH PERIODS: AFDC SAMPLE

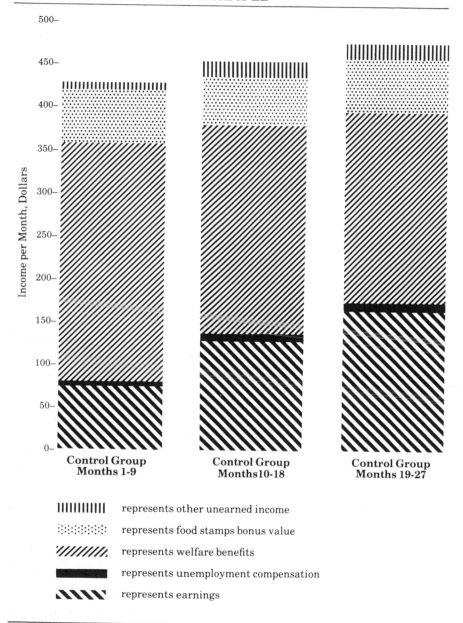

‖‖‖‖‖‖‖‖	represents other unearned income
::::::::::	represents food stamps bonus value
///////	represents welfare benefits
▬▬▬▬	represents unemployment compensation
◣◣◣◣	represents earnings

The control group yielded data that helped to shed light on other programs seeking to increase employment among women on welfare. The most substantial of these programs is the Work Incentive Program (WIN), which began in 1967 and which requires local welfare agencies to screen welfare recipients for employability and to provide employment counseling and training. Over the years the emphasis in the program has shifted, placing greater weight on public service employment and on placement into unsubsidized jobs. In contrast to supported work, the WIN program requires employable welfare recipients to accept services. Those who do not accept them may face cuts or even termination of their welfare benefits. This mandatory character of the WIN program is of particular interest, for almost all of the control group in the supported work study, by virtue of the supported work eligibility criteria, would be termed employable by WIN and therefore subject to WIN sanctions.

In addition to WIN, some welfare participants in recent years have had access to assistance in obtaining training and jobs through the Comprehensive Employment and Training Act (CETA). A number of local governments also have made special efforts to hire welfare recipients. These efforts at job development and placement played a significant role in the employment of members of the control group. In each of the three 9-month periods, about 18 percent to 22 percent of the control group's earnings came from jobs connected with either CETA or WIN, and when one adds other government jobs, that share rises to about one-third of their earnings. However, this percentage did not increase substantially over the period of the study. It was roughly the same in each of the three time segments when interviews were held. Thus, the overall rise in employment among the AFDC controls over the entire period must be attributed to factors unrelated to public service or government job availability.

This brief review of the employment and welfare income experience of the control group provides the context in which the supported work program operated for members of the AFDC group. The trends that emerged point up the importance of the experimental design: the control group findings tell what would have happened to the participants in the program had they not had the experience of supported work. In the ensuing discussion of the effects of supported work, the differences in the experience of participants and controls must be seen against a background in which the employment situation of the controls was continuously improving. This is of fundamental importance in identifying differences attributable to the supported work experience and in isolating these from changes that would have occurred anyway because of general economic trends affecting both experimentals and controls.

SUPPORTED WORK'S EFFECTS
ON EMPLOYMENT

The employment effects of the supported work program on members of the AFDC target group are summarized in Figure 4-5, showing total hours worked for both experimentals and controls, as well as the average number of hours that the experimentals worked while in the program. The program was bound to have an effect in the initial months, for members of the experimental group were offered an opportunity for a full-time job when they became participants, whereas members of the control group had no such opportunity.

Figure 4-5

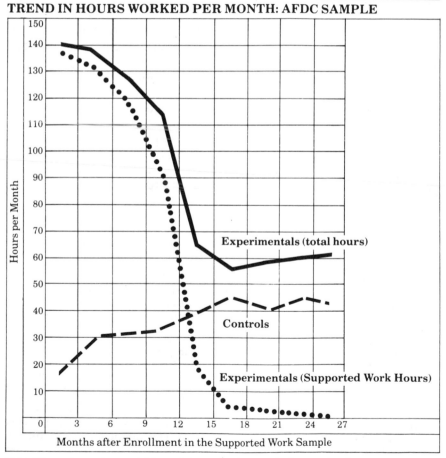

TREND IN HOURS WORKED PER MONTH: AFDC SAMPLE

Note: All experimental-control differentials are significant at the 5 percent level.

Thus, the initial difference in hours worked is not surprising. The magnitude of the difference, however, is significant[3] and reflects the fact that, as noted in Chapter 2, the AFDC group on the average stayed in the program two to three months longer than did the other target groups.[4] This difference is the clearest indicator that the AFDC participants found the supported work experience easier to adjust to, and more rewarding, than did the other target groups.

As can be seen from Figure 4-5, the hours worked by the AFDC experimentals declined as they left the program. The sharpest decline began in the tenth month, reflecting the high rate of program termination during months 10 to 12 when the experimentals approached the maximum stay in the program.

In Tables 4-1, 4-2, and 4-3, data are presented on the percentage of the individuals in the sample who were employed, the number of hours they worked and the earnings of the control and experimental groups, as well as the differences between the two groups. These data show that in every period the experimentals did better than the controls—in terms of the employment rate, of hours worked, and of earnings. The difference between experimentals and controls was statistically significant in all cases—in spite of the fact that the control group, because of improving conditions in the economy during the study, was steadily bettering its employment and earnings record.

Because a stated objective of supported work was to facilitate the movement of participants into the regular labor market, the most eagerly awaited data were those documenting participants' experiences after they "graduated" from the program. Thus, the

---

3. Throughout this document, experimental and control differences are called significant only if there is a small probability—usually no more than 1 chance in 20—that they were the result of chance rather than a program effect. For example, there is only a 0.05 probability that experimental-control differences marked with a dagger in Table 4-1 would have occurred in the absence of actual differences existing in the means of the populations from which the participant and control samples were drawn. Because of the larger probability that they may have occurred by chance, experimental-control differences that cannot be statistically distinguished from zero and that are not marked with an asterisk or a dagger should be interpreted with caution.

4. The data on average length of stay in the program in Chapter 2 were for all participants at all 15 sites. However, the figures are very similar for the research sample at 10 sites. The supported work demonstration included a planned variation in the maximum length of stay in the program: 12 or 18 months at different sites. The results show that this did not have an impact on the average length of stay of individuals in any of the four target groups. However, there is some indication of a benefit to the AFDC group from the longer programs in that the rate of mandatory graduation was much lower at the 18-month than at the 12-month sites.

Table 4–1. Percent Employed per 3-Month Follow-Up Period: AFDC Sample

Month After Enrollment in the Sample	Experimental Group Mean	Control Group Mean	Experimental-Control Differential	Mean for	
				Experimentals With Any Supported Work Job[a]	Experimentals With Only Supported Work Jobs[a]
1–3	95.2	19.4	75.8†	93.6[b]	92.2
4–6	89.0	26.0	63.0†	85.4	82.3
7–9	82.4	28.2	54.2†	75.2	71.9
10–12	73.5	27.5	46.0†	59.0	52.9
13–15	58.4	31.7	26.7†	32.9	24.9
16–18	40.4	35.1	5.3†	4.3	3.4
19–21	41.4	33.3	8.1†	2.9	2.6
22–24	42.3	34.9	7.4*	1.3	0.6
25–27	42.0	34.9	7.1*	0.0	0.0

Source: Interviews conducted between February 1976 and March 1979 with experimentals and controls at seven of the supported work sites. The first 18 months of data are for the sample of 1,351 individuals who completed the baseline, 9- and 18-month interviews; the data on months 19 through 27 are from the 620 individuals who completed 27-month interviews.

Notes: The data presented in the first three columns are regression-adjusted estimates that control the differences of age, sex, race, education, prior work experience, household composition, site, and length of site operation.

[a]These data are not regression adjusted. No experimentals should have been in the program beyond month 21. The small number indicated as participating after that time reflects either data errors or failures by program operators to terminate individuals on schedule.

[b]Of the experimentals, 2.9 percent never showed up for their supported work jobs, and another 3.7 percent were in the program for less than 30 days. Because employment intervals of less than 2 weeks were not recorded in interviews, the percentages in this table may actually slightly understate program participation.

†Statistically significant at the 5 percent level.

*Statistically significant at the 10 percent level.

Table 4-2. Average Hours Worked per Month, by Length of Follow-Up: AFDC Sample

Month After Enrollment in the Sample	Experimental Group Mean	Control Group Mean	Experimental-Control Differential	Mean Hours in Supported Work[a]	
				Hours	As Percent of Total Hours of Experimentals
1–3	140.3	17.8	122.5†	137.6	98.1
4–6	138.6	30.7	107.9†	131.7	95.0
7–9	127.5	33.1	94.4†	116.3	91.2
10–12	114.0	35.1	78.9†	89.2	78.2
13–15	65.5	40.6	24.9†	21.6	33.0
16–18	56.1	46.0	10.1†	4.8	8.6
19–21	59.4	42.9	16.5†	3.6	6.1
22–24	61.2	46.0	15.2†	1.0	1.6
25–27	61.8	45.9	15.9†	0.0	0.0

Source: See Table 4–1.

Notes: The data presented in the first three columns are regression-adjusted estimates that control for differences of age, sex, race, education, prior work experience, household composition, site, and length of site operation. Averages are calculated for all members of the sample, including those with no employment in the covered period.

[a]These data are not regression adjusted. No experimentals should have been in the program beyond month 21. The small number indicated as participating after that time reflects either data errors or failures by program operators to terminate individuals on schedule.

†Statistically significant at the 5 percent level.

Table 4-3. Average Earnings per Month, by Length of Follow-Up: AFDC Sample

Month After Enrollment in the Sample	Experimental Group Mean	Control Group Mean	Experimental-Control Differential	Mean Earnings From Supported Work[a]	
				Earnings	As Percent of Total Earnings of Experimentals
1–3	$409.44	$49.28	$360.16†	$401.27	98.0
4–6	412.30	90.84	321.46†	389.01	94.4
7–9	387.20	99.28	287.92†	348.51	90.0
10–12	371.25	117.85	253.40†	275.45	74.2
13–15	237.11	140.12	96.99†	65.76	27.7
16–18	213.30	159.33	53.97†	13.99	6.6
19–21	230.92	161.79	69.13†	10.97	4.8
22–24	244.64	166.54	78.10†	2.93	1.2
25–27	248.47	167.86	80.61†	0.00	0.0

Source: See Table 4-1.

Notes: The data presented in the first three columns are regression-adjusted estimates that control for differences of age, sex, race, education, prior work experience, household composition, site, and length of site operation. Averages are calculated for all members of the sample, including those with no employment in the covered period. Dollar amounts reported are gross earnings unadjusted for inflation.

aThese data are not regression adjusted. No experimentals should have been in the program beyond month 21. The small number indicated as participating after that time reflects either data errors or failures by program operators to terminate individuals on schedule.

†Statistically significant at the 5 percent level.

figures for the period beginning 16 months after entry into the program are of key importance. By that time, almost all participants had left the program.[5] The figures show that the differences between experimentals and controls in employment rates, hours, and earnings were considerably reduced, yet persisted to statistically significant degrees. In addition, the differential in hours worked between the experimental and control groups continued at approximately the same level from the sixteenth month on. This led to the finding that differences in employment rates, hours worked, and earnings are likely to continue into the future. What is not known is whether the magnitude of the differential will remain the same. To shed light on this, a follow-up study is currently going on.

The positive post-program effects reflected in Tables 4-1, 4-2, and 4-3 show that the experimentals not only achieved a higher rate of employment, but also worked more hours and attained higher wage rates. Thus, in months 25-27, the experimental group's employment rate was 20 percent above that of the controls; hours worked were 35 percent higher; and earnings exceeded those of the controls by almost 50 percent. The program therefore appears to have had an impact not only on employment as such, but also on the quality of employment. Evidence of this effect is also reflected in the data on wage rates in Table 4-4. This table shows that during the period when the experimentals were employed in supported work programs, there was little difference between their wage rates and those of the controls. After month 12, as larger numbers of participants left supported work, the difference between wage rates of experimentals and controls began to rise. From month 16 on, the wage rates of the experimentals who worked ranged from 12 to 38 cents an hour more than those of controls.

The interpretation of this pattern of employment effects for the AFDC group depends on the answer to a number of questions, the most critical of which is whether the longer term impacts that are measured only for the half of the sample followed for 27 months are typical of what would have been expected had the full sample been followed that long. A second area of inquiry is whether the program was equally effective among all the participants or of particular benefit for certain subsets of this group. The final questions concern additional possible explanations of the experimental-control differential: the extent to which it was affected by the high receipt of unemployment compensation by the experimentals or the avail-

5. As noted earlier, participants at some sites were permitted to spend up to 18 months in the program (with additional elapsed time allowed for leave from the program for health or other reasons).

Table 4-4. Average Hourly Wage Rates of Those Employed, by Length of Follow-Up: AFDC Sample

Month After Enrollment in the Sample	Experimental Group Mean	Control Group Mean	Nonprogram Wage Rates of Experimentals	Program Wage Rates of Experimentals	
				Wage Rate	As Percent of Nonprogram Wage Rate
1–3	$2.92	$2.77	$3.03	$2.92	96.4
4–6	2.97	2.96	3.38	2.95	87.3
7–9	3.04	3.00	3.44	3.00	87.2
10–12	3.26	3.36	3.86	3.09	80.1
13–15	3.62	3.45	3.90	3.04	77.9
16–18	3.80	3.46	3.89	2.91	74.8
19–21	3.89	3.77	3.94	3.05[a]	77.4
22–24	4.00	3.62	4.02	2.93[a]	72.9
25–27	4.01	3.66	4.01	—	—

Source: See Table 4-1.

Notes: The data in this table are not regression adjusted. The wage rate figures are calculated by dividing the average earnings in the given period by average hours. Because these differences are based on aggregate data, significance tests were not available.

[a]These data are based on very small sample sizes. No experimentals were employed in supported work programs beyond month 24.

ability of other subsidized job opportunities to either the experimentals or controls.

In addressing the question of the representativeness of the responses for the 19- through 27-month period, data on the earlier months were examined separately for the two sample cohorts: those followed for only 18 months, and those followed for the full 27 months after their enrollment in the sample. This comparison indicates a pattern that was common to the other target groups: supported work seems to have had its largest impacts on those individuals enrolled earliest (in this case, the 27-month cohort). Moreover, this was primarily the result of greater employment among those controls entering the sample at later dates rather than of any difference in the behavior of the experimentals in the two cohorts. Several explanations for this variation were examined. It does not seem to be the result either of differences in the measured background characteristics of individuals in the two samples or of any change in the sites from which the two samples were drawn. A more probable explanation lies in improvements in the labor market that occurred over the life of the demonstration: both the continuing decline in the unemployment rate and the increase in government employment programs over this period.

The variation in the estimate of supported work's impacts between the two cohorts suggests that program effects may be sensitive to the environment in which the program is implemented. However, under the particular conditions faced by the supported work sample, reasonable assumptions about the future behavior of the 18-month cohort lead to the overall conclusion that experimental-control differences for the full sample, had it been followed, might have been smaller than those observed for the 27-month cohort, but would still have been statistically significant. The supplemental AFDC survey conducted in late 1979 will allow a further examination of these issues.

On the second question, the evidence, although not strong, suggests that supported work's longer term impacts were particularly large among certain subsets of the target population: older women (those between 36 and 44 at their enrollment in the program) and women who had not completed high school, who had been on welfare for a particularly long period of time, who had no prior work experience, or who had not recently participated in a job-training program. In a pattern that is similar to the other target groups and also to the cohort findings, the subgroups of the sample that appear to be most affected by supported work are those that have relatively low levels of employment in the absence of the program, as revealed by the behavior of the control group.[6]

The third aspect of the employment experience of experimentals and controls that deserves attention relates to unemployment insurance. In general, supported workers did not qualify for unemployment insurance because the program did not pay the unemployment insurance tax on behalf of their participants. In New York City, however, the state law required that unemployment tax be paid. This meant that experimentals having been steadily employed in supported work had a higher degree of eligibility for unemployment insurance than the less steadily working controls. As it turned out in follow-up interviews, this indeed was the case: the experimental group in New York received unemployment compensation for an average of over 2 months, compared to less than half a month for the controls.

Unemployment compensation supports people while they are out of work, giving them the chance to look for a job for a longer period of time than they might if they did not receive such assistance. The availability of unemployment compensation thus eased the pressure on the experimentals to locate a job quickly and might have caused them to have worked less in the immediate aftermath of leaving the program than the controls. In the long run, of course, the longer and more selective job search might well help these individuals to land better and better paying jobs.

Access to unemployment compensation for supported workers was not entirely limited to the New York site, however, because during the period of the recession in 1975 through 1977, a special unemployment assistance program was made available by the federal government. This permitted individuals who had been in jobs where unemployment insurance taxes were not paid to qualify for special unemployment assistance (SUA). Thus, supported workers in some sites were able to qualify for benefits under SUA by virtue of their months of employment in supported work. Receipt of SUA was uneven across sites, however, because of local variations in the interpretation of supported work as an employment or training program and/or because of differences in the degree to which supported work program operators facilitated access to SUA for their participants.

6. In addition, for this and other target groups there was a large variation in program impacts at the various sites, although this does not follow a consistent pattern across target groups or appear to be clearly related to any known differences in program design or to local labor market conditions.

Overall, in months 10 to 18, about 23 percent of the experimental AFDC group received unemployment compensation, whereas only 3 percent of the control group did. In months 19 to 27, 9 percent of the experimentals received unemployment compensation as compared to 2 percent for the control group.

The question is what the employment differential between experimentals and controls would have been had unemployment compensation not been available to the supported workers. The evidence from the supported work study suggests that the supported workers would have worked more and the difference between them and the controls would have been correspondingly greater. This was so, particularly in months 10 to 18 when unemployment compensation was highest and therefore the pressure on the experimentals to find a job least strong. It is clear, therefore, that the availability of unemployment aid probably served to reduce the extent of employment differences between experimentals and controls.

Table 4–5. Employment in CETA, WIN, and Public Sector Jobs: AFDC Sample

Type of Job	Months 1–9		Months 10–18		Months 19–27	
	Experi-mentals	Con-trols	Experi-mentals	Con-trols	Experi-mentals	Con-trols
Percent with CETA or WIN job	1.6	7.7	5.7	8.3	8.1	5.3
Percent of nonprogram earnings from CETA or WIN job[a]	19.5	22.2	11.4	22.2	16.2	18.5
Percent with CETA, WIN, or government job	3.1	10.5	15.8	12.5	21.1	10.2
Percent of nonprogram earnings from CETA, WIN, or government job[a]	34.3	31.2	40.4	35.7	46.8	30.5

Source: See Table 4–1.

Notes: The data in this table are simple subgroup means and are not regression adjusted. No tests of statistical significance were computed. To categorize a job, respondents were asked whether or not a specific job was for state or local government, and whether or not it was part of a special government employment program such as CETA or WIN.

[a]These percentages are calculated from experimental and control group means for earnings from CETA or WIN or from CETA, WIN, or government jobs and total earnings.

Finally, both the experimentals and the controls were affected by the availability of public sector jobs. Table 4-5 shows separately the extent to which the AFDC experimentals and controls obtained jobs that they identified as CETA or WIN subsidized as well as employment in all public sector jobs. Overall, there is no evidence that the post-program impact on the AFDC sample was the result of supported work participants being placed in other subsidized employment. During the first 18 months, a comparison between experimentals and controls can be discounted because many experimentals were still in the program. During months 19 through 27, there is little difference between the two groups in CETA or WIN jobs, but Table 4-5 does indicate that there are substantial differences between experimentals and controls in employment in unsubsidized government jobs. This suggests that one of the ways in which supported work resulted in increased employment was through the greater employment of experimentals than controls in the public sector.

SUPPORTED WORK'S EFFECTS ON WELFARE AND TOTAL INCOME

Supported work increased the earnings of participants both during their stay in the program and, to a lesser extent, after they left it. When their earnings increased, their payments from welfare and food stamps went down, because that is the way these programs are designed. Figure 4-6 shows the trends in combined welfare and food stamp income for the AFDC group. This figure is to some degree the mirror image of the figure on hours worked in the previous section. The experimentals' food stamp and welfare income declined through month 10 and then began to rise as they left supported work and their earnings decreased.[7] The experimental-control difference in welfare and food stamp income was greatest in months 4 to 6, when it was about $138: by months 25 to 27 the difference had declined to $55.

Table 4-6 shows both the amount of income experimentals and controls received from various sources and the percentage receiving such income. Throughout the 27-month period, more controls than experimentals received welfare benefits, and by months 19 through

7. The supported work effect on experimentals' welfare and food stamp income did not occur completely in the first period, because it took some time for the welfare agencies to redetermine participants' income and adjust their welfare payments. Thus, the experimentals' welfare and food stamp income continued to fall in the first 6 months.

Figure 4-6

TREND IN RECEIPT OF WELFARE INCOME AND FOOD STAMP BONUSES: AFDC SAMPLE

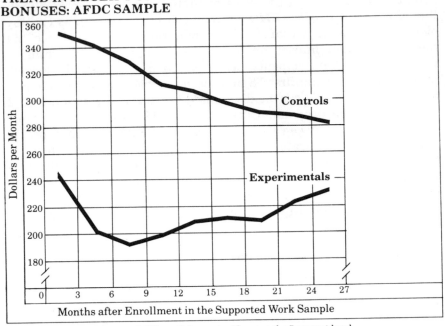

Note: All experimental-control differentials are significant at the 5 percent level.

27, about twice as many experimentals as controls had left the AFDC rolls (71 percent of the experimentals received welfare payments compared to 85 percent of the controls). In addition, the average welfare benefits for those experimentals left on the rolls were lower than those for controls. As a result, the overall average for experimentals in the first 9 months was $170 a month compared to $278 a month for the controls. By months 19 through 27, the controls were still receiving an average of $52 a month more than the experimentals. Supplemental data also indicate that experimentals received significantly fewer Medicaid benefits; they also paid higher rentals in public housing projects than did members of the control group.[8]

Table 4-6 also provides a picture of the relationship between total income and its components. Whereas in months 1 through 9 the

8. Among the almost 40 percent of experimentals and controls living in public housing throughout the 27-month study period, the experimentals paid significantly more rent ($5 to $15 per month) than the controls in each 9-month period.

Table 4-6. Percent Receiving Income from Various Sources during 9-Month Periods and Average Monthly Income Received: AFDC Sample

Source of Income	Months 1-9		Months 10-18		Months 19-27	
	Experimental-Control Differential	Control Group Mean	Experimental-Control Differential	Control Group Mean	Experimental-Control Differential	Control Group Mean
	Percent Receiving					
Earnings	59.8†	36.5	37.1†	39.4	8.5†	40.6
Unearned income						
Unemployment compensation	-1.0	2.0	20.1†	3.0	7.2†	2.0
Welfare[a]	-3.9†	97.7	-7.7†	90.1	-13.7†	85.1
Food stamps	-8.5†	94.6	-12.4†	85.9	-15.1†	82.3
Other[b]	-7.0†	15.7	-3.0*	11.4	-1.4	12.2
Percent with Medicaid Card	0.7	95.4	-9.6†	86.5	-9.2†	80.6
	Average Monthly Amount[d]					
All sources[c]	$192.96†	$435.10	$70.03†	$454.44	$27.36	$470.14
Earnings	322.16†	78.28	142.98†	131.08	77.01†	165.88
Unearned income						
Unemployment compensation	-1.77†	2.20	27.39†	3.67	9.44†	2.91
Welfare[a]	-108.08†	277.90	-82.32†	246.60	-51.94†	224.00
Food Stamp Bonus Value[e]	-18.63†	63.46	-15.87†	58.02	-13.11†	60.25
Other[b]	-2.08	14.04	-4.05	16.05	3.58	18.30
Welfare benefits, recipients only ($)[a,f]	-103.40	284.44	-74.33	273.70	-22.25	263.22

Source: See Table 4-1.

Notes: All data are regression adjusted.

[a]Welfare includes AFDC, GA, SSI, and other unspecified cash welfare income.

[b]Other unearned income includes Social Security, pensions, alimony, and child support.

[c]"All Sources" includes earned and unearned income, as itemized in the table, and does not include the value of Medicaid or other in-kind benefits.

[d]Averages are calculated including individuals receiving zero benefits.

[e]Represents the difference between the purchase price of the food stamps and their face value.

[f]Excludes individuals receiving zero benefits. Significance tests were not performed on these data.

†Statistically significant at the 5 percent level.

*Statistically significant at the 10 percent level.

earnings of the experimentals were $322 per month higher than those of the controls, their total income was $193 higher. The total income differences between the experimentals and controls were large and statistically significant in periods 1 through 9 and 10 through 18. By months 19 to 27 the difference was still positive, but small and no longer statistically significant.

One other interesting way to look at total income figures is in terms of the percentage of families with incomes below the poverty level. These data are reported in Table 4-7. The immediate effect of the supported work program was to reduce substantially the number of experimentals and their families in poverty and to raise the average income level of the participants considerably above the poverty level. Thus, whereas 53 percent of the control group families had incomes below the poverty level during months 1 through 9, this was true for only 12 percent of the experimentals (i.e., a difference of 41.5 percent). Once supported workers had left the program, however, the experimental-control differentials declined substantially but not all the way. Thus, in months 19 to 27, when almost all participants were out of the program, the percentage of experimentals' families with incomes below the poverty level was still somewhat smaller than the controls', although not significantly so.

Table 4-6 makes clear that the experimental-control differential in earnings is considerably larger than the experimental-control differential in total income. In part, this is due to a reduction in welfare payments. For example, over the first 9-month period, the welfare and food stamp benefits of both experimentals and controls were cut by an average of about one-third of their earnings gains. In subsequent periods, however, this relatively small difference in income between experimentals and controls, as distinct from the larger earnings differential, is not as readily explained. It is attributable to a combination of changing earnings patterns among those receiving and no longer receiving welfare, and to changes in unemployment compensation.

In isolation these data would appear to have considerable welfare policy importance because they relate to concerns about work incentives for people whose benefits are reduced as earnings increase. It is important, therefore, to go beyond these data to figures presented in Table 4-8 for months 25 to 27. They show that if, in fact, there is employment for these groups, their total income is substantially higher. It is true that the increased earnings of the employed experimentals and the employed controls led to a less than equivalent increase in total income. But the increase is substantial nonetheless.

Table 4-7. Total Income in Relationship to the Poverty Level, by Length of Follow-Up: AFDC Sample

Item	Months 1–9 Experimental-Control Differential	Months 1–9 Control Group Mean	Months 10–18 Experimental-Control Differential	Months 10–18 Control Group Mean	Months 19–27 Experimental-Control Differential	Months 19–27 Control Group Mean
Percent of families with income below the poverty level	-41.5†	53.4	-17.9†	54.9	-2.3	53.5
Average income as a percent of the poverty level	50.2†	104.5	16.8†	105.5	3.0	111.2

Source: See Table 4-1.

Notes: These data are based on (1) the reported income only of the respondents to the interviews (and not of other members of the households) and (2) the relationship and ages of only the immediate family members (spouse and children) as reported in the interviews. The poverty level income thresholds used for families with various combinations of head of household, family size, and number of children under 18 were as reported in *Current Population Reports: Consumer Income*, Washington, D.C.: U.S. Department of Commerce, Bureau of the Census, July 1978 (Table A.2). For comparison purposes, incomes of sample members were adjusted by the GNP Index (reported in *Business Conditions Digest*, 17 (1) (January 1977) and 19 (2) (February 1979) to constant fourth-quarter 1976 dollars.

†Statistically significant at the 5 percent level.

Table 4-8. Average Monthly Total Income by Employment Status, Months 25 to 27: AFDC Sample

Group	Employed	Unemployed
Experimentals	$700.82	$351.89
Controls	$651.47	$381.05

Source: See Table 4-1.
Note: The data in this table are not regression adjusted.

The tax system introduces another inducement not to work. Increased earnings are subject to income and Social Security taxes, and certain special benefits not included in cash welfare payments, such as Medicaid, are also reduced. Taking these further subtractions from total income into account, the increase in after-tax real income is somewhat less than 50 percent of the difference in before-tax earnings of the employed and unemployed. The essential point is that experimentals and controls face similar disincentives, but their employment rate still increases steadily.

Table 4-8 also shows that there is a difference in the total income of the unemployed experimentals and the unemployed controls. Part of this difference is due to a 6-percentage-point differential in welfare participation. There is some evidence that experimentals who have been employed and who become unemployed go back on welfare at a slower rate than do controls. It is not clear over the longer term whether this phenomenon will persist. It may be that unemployed experimentals still searching for jobs have delayed re-applying for welfare while they still have some hope in the short term of finding another job. Continued differentials in unemployment compensation may also affect the experimentals' behavior. However, this differential in welfare payments between unemployed experimentals and unemployed controls is likely to become smaller as time goes on. If so, this would mean that the total income of the experimentals as a group would rise relative to the total income of the controls as welfare payments of the experimentals rise, and that this impact of supported work in the form of decreased public assistance costs would lessen.

SUPPORTED WORK'S EFFECTS ON CHILD CARE

AFDC women are on welfare because they have dependent children and low income. The eligibility criteria of supported work barred women who had children under 6 years of age. Still, as these women go to work, arrangements have to be made for child care during after-school hours and vacations. Table 4-9 provides information on work-related child care for the women in the sample with children under 13 years of age. Overall in each of the 9-month periods, the experimentals used significantly more child care services than did the controls. Paralleling the experience with AFDC women in general, the AFDC mothers in this sample made little use of formal day care programs. Most of the child care services they used were provided in the home of the participant or in someone else's home. This was true for both the experimentals and the controls.

There is a substantial difference over the first 18 months between the responses of the controls and those of the experimentals about the importance of child care. A higher percentage of controls than experimentals cited the nonavailability of child care as a reason for not working. Based on this difference, it is possible to speculate that if these respondents were offered a concrete employment opportunity such as supported work, they would have been able to deal with their child care problems.

CONCLUSION

Participation in supported work for the AFDC target group led to an increase in the employment rate, hours worked, and earnings for the experimentals, both while they were in the program and after they had left it. The impacts were larger during the first 9 months, when most of the experimentals had a supported work job, but the differences continued at statistically significant levels into the post-program period. There was also a significant reduction in welfare dependency among experimentals. As a result of their higher earnings, the AFDC participants received substantially less income from the AFDC and food stamp programs. By months 19 through 27, about twice as many experimentals as controls had left the AFDC rolls.

There is some indication that the program had an impact not only on the employment rate of the experimentals, but also on the quality of employment. From month 16 on, the wage rates of the experimentals who worked ranged from 12 to 38 cents an hour more than those of controls. Evidence also suggests that supported work's longer term impacts may have been particularly large among certain subsets of the target population: older women (those between 36 and 44 at their enrollment), women who had not completed high school, who had been on welfare for a long period of

Table 4-9. Use of Work-Related Child Care by the Subsample of AFDC Respondents with Children under 13 Years, by Length of Follow-Up

Child Care Measures	Months 1-9		Months 10-18		Months 19-27	
	Experimental-Control Differential	Control Group Mean	Experimental-Control Differential	Control Group Mean	Experimental-Control Differential	Control Group Mean
Percent who used child care services[a]	35.5†	12.7	17.5†	11.3	4.5†	6.7
Day care center[a]	3.0	0.7	1.7	0.6	1.0	0.3
Care in own home[a]	15.9	7.1	4.7	5.9	0.6	3.0
Care in other's home[a]	19.9	8.2	13.0	7.5	4.4	4.3
Average No. months used	3.0†	0.5	0.9†	0.7	0.3	0.4
Percent reporting no child care reason for not working[b]	-23.5†	33.4	-6.1†	31.0	-1.1	24.6
Percent of AFDC sample with children under 13 years	76.8		72.4		64.9	

Source: See Table 4-1.

Notes: Those with no children under 13 years were assumed not to need work-related child care. The data in this table are not regression adjusted.

[a]Items may add to a number greater than the total because multiple types of services may have been used.

[b]During at least part of the period.

†Statistically significant at the 5 percent level.

time, who had no prior work experience, or who had not recently participated in a job-training program.

The results of the benefit-cost analysis, discussed in a later chapter, show that the impacts for this target group are substantial enough so that, overall, the benefits exceed the costs.

Chapter 5

Findings for the Ex-Addict Target Group

This chapter summarizes the findings on the effects of the supported work program on members of the ex-addict target group.[1] It is based on interviews with experimentals and controls over a 36-month period at four of the local sites. These findings show that, while they were in the program, the experimentals worked more, received less public assistance, and committed fewer criminal activities than the nonparticipating controls. They also suggest that this decrease in criminal activity persisted into the post-program period. For a subset of the sample followed up by the researchers for the full 36 months, there is also evidence of a post-program employment gain, but this is less conclusive. Finally, there is no indication that supported work significantly affected the drug use of this group of ex-addicts either during the period when they participated in the program or afterward.

The first section of this chapter briefly describes the employment experience, drug use, and criminal activities of the control group during the period of the study. The subsequent sections contrast the behavior of the controls with that of the experimentals in order to assess the program's impact.

---

1. The findings are presented in full in a forthcoming report by Katherine Dickinson with Rebecca Maynard, *The Impact of Supported Work on Ex-Addicts*, MDRC, 1980.

EMPLOYMENT, DRUG USE, AND CRIMINAL ACTIVITY OF THE CONTROL GROUP

Over the period covered by the study, employment among controls tended to increase, and both drug use and arrests—indicators of involvement in crime—tended to decrease. Figure 5-1 shows a graph of the hours worked by the control group members from the time of their enrollment in the sample through the subsequent 36 months. During the first 6 months after random assignment, employment among controls rose from 0 to 47 hours per month, and it continued to increase, although at a slower rate, throughout the first 2 years. During the third year, employment fell somewhat. A comparison of the hours worked by the ex-addict control group with those of the other target groups indicates that they worked more than the AFDC group but less than the ex-offenders and youths (see Figure 4-2).

The initial rise in the employment level of the controls was due to two factors. Particularly during the first 6-month period, a large portion of the increase was attributable to individuals who, because

Figure 5-1

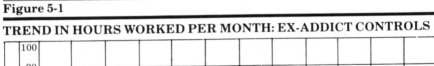

TREND IN HOURS WORKED PER MONTH: EX-ADDICT CONTROLS

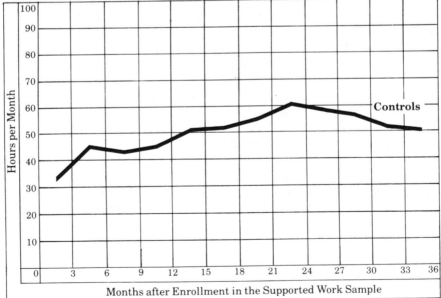

of program eligibility criteria, were unemployed at the time they were enrolled in the sample. They then gradually reached their "typical" employment level—a phenomenon previously referred to as regression to the mean. The second factor is the improving labor market during the period of the study. Estimates are that roughly 20 percent of the total change in hours was attributable to this improvement in the labor market and 80 percent to the regression to the mean.

The decrease in controls' employment from about 60 to 50 hours per month during months 25 to 36 is more complex. The graph presented in Figure 5–1 combines information from interviews with all of the members of the control group: those followed for only 18 months (the 18-month cohort), those followed for only 27 months (the 27-month cohort), and those followed for the full 36 months (the 36-month cohort). Because of this change in sample, what looks like a decrease in employment is in fact primarily explained by the fact that the 36-month cohort worked less than the other two cohorts during much of the study period.

Drug use among controls was quite prevalent; during the first 9-month period 38 percent of the controls reported the use of some drug other than alcohol or marijuana, and 22 percent reported the continued or renewed use of heroin. Over the subsequent 9-month time periods the percentage reporting use of any drug declined quite steadily, with only about 21 percent reporting any use during months 28 to 36. Two factors contribute to this change. First, there was a decline nationally in drug use during the calendar year 1978, the period when this lower use was reported; and second, the later enrollees in the supported work program were higher drug users than were the early ones.

The incidence of arrests among the ex-addict controls was also high during the period of the study. About 19 percent of the control group members reported having been arrested during each of the first three 9-month periods, and 14 percent were arrested during months 28 to 36. (As with the employment and drug-use results, at least a partial explanation for this trend in arrest rates is the changing sample.) Because these data include multiple arrests of the same individuals, it is also useful to examine the number of members of the control group arrested over the full period of the study. Cumulatively, during the first 18 months after enrollment, 34 percent of the controls had been arrested at least once and, among those followed for the full 36-month period, over half reported having been arrested during the three years since their enrollment. Between 20 and 25 percent of those arrested reported having been charged with a robbery, and a similar percentage reported having been charged with a drug offense.

This brief review of the experience of the ex-addict control group indicates the environment in which supported work operated. Overall, the ex-addicts had more hours of employment than did the AFDC controls, but they appear to have benefited less from improvements over time in the labor market. In the absence of any program intervention, the controls' behavior suggests that this group would continue to show a substantial incidence of drug use and criminal activity. In the next sections the behavior of the supported work participants is examined against the background of this portrait of what would have occurred in the absence of the program.

SUPPORTED WORK'S EFFECT ON EMPLOYMENT

The impact of supported work on the employment of members of the ex-addict target group is summarized in Figure 5-2, which shows the average hours worked per month by the experimentals and the controls, as well as the average hours that the experimentals worked in the supported work program itself. During the first few months following enrollment, as a result of their program jobs, the employment gains of the experimentals were substantial. (As noted in Chapter 2, the ex-addicts stayed an average of almost 7 months in the program.) However, these gains decreased sharply as the experimentals left supported work. By months 16 to 18, when only 5 percent of the experimentals were still in supported work, there was essentially no difference in the overall employment levels of the two groups. The similarity in experimentals' and controls' employment persisted over a 9-month period, after which experimentals tended to increase their hours of employment while that of controls decreased. The difference in the hours worked (5 to 10 per month) during months 25 to 30 was not statistically significant, but became rather large and significant (20 hours per month) in months 31 to 36. In that period the experimentals worked an average of over 70 hours per month compared to the controls' 50 hours.

In general, a similar pattern was observed for employment rates, hours of work, and earnings, as seen from the data presented in Tables 5-1, 5-2, and 5-3. As shown in Table 5-1, 92 percent of the experimentals were employed in the first 3 months following enrollment, but this percentage fell to between 40 and 49 percent for the 3-month periods following month 18. This showing was not significantly above that of the controls, except in the final 3 months,

Figure 5-2

TREND IN HOURS WORKED PER MONTH: EX-ADDICT SAMPLE

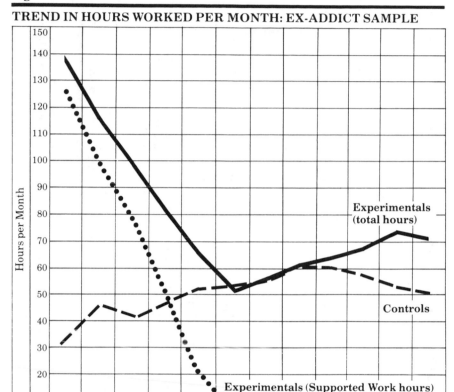

Months after Enrollment in the Supported Work Sample

Note: Experimental-control differentials are significant at the 5 percent level for
months 1 to 15 and 31 to 36.

when 49 percent of the experimentals were employed compared to
only 32 percent of the controls. Similarly, Table 5-3 shows that the
difference between the monthly earnings of experimentals and
controls fell from $273 in months 1 through 3 to insignificant levels
in months 16 through 30. It increased thereafter to about $100 a
month, with experimentals earnings $318 a month and controls
$218, in months 34 to 36. The differentials in earnings were small
when compared to those in the number of hours worked during
months 1 through 15. This is because the program's wage rates,
which accounted for the bulk of the experimentals' earnings in that

Table 5-1.   Percent Employed per 3-Month Follow-Up Period: Ex-Addict Sample

Month After Enrollment in the Sample	Experimental Group Mean	Control Group Mean	Experimental-Control Differential	Mean for	
				Experimentals With Any Supported Work Job[a]	Experimentals With Only Supported Work Jobs[a]
1-3	91.7	30.9	60.8†	86.1[b]	80.8
4-6	76.8	39.0	37.8†	66.3	61.4
7-9	67.2	37.1	30.1†	52.7	47.5
10-12	54.5	36.4	18.1†	33.9	29.8
13-15	50.6	40.4	10.2†	20.3	15.5
16-18	39.4	40.0	-0.6	5.3	3.3
19-21	40.0	40.4	-0.4	1.7	1.5
22-24	43.0	43.4	-0.4	0.9	0.7
25-27	45.4	43.0	2.4	0.2	0.2
28-30	42.0	37.8	4.2	0.0	0.0
31-33	47.2	38.7	8.5	0.0	0.0
34-36	48.8	31.6	17.2†	0.0	0.0

Source: Interviews conducted between April 1975 and March 1979 with experimentals and controls at four of the supported work sites. The first 18 months of data are for the sample of 974 individuals who completed the baseline, 9- and 18-month interviews; the data on months 19 through 27 are from the 885 individuals who completed 27-month interviews; the data on months 28 through 36 are from the 317 individuals who completed 36-month interviews.

Notes: The data presented in the first three columns are regression-adjusted estimates that control for differences of age, sex, race, education, prior work experience, household composition, site, and length of site operation.

aThese data are not regression adjusted. No experimentals should have been in the program beyond month 21. The small number indicated as participating after that time reflects either data errors or failures by program operators to terminate individuals on schedule.

bOf the experimentals, 5.1 percent never showed up for their supported work jobs and another 9.1 percent were in the program for less than 30 days. Because employment intervals of less than two weeks were not recorded in interviews, the percentages in this table may actually slightly understate program participation.

†Statistically significant at the 5 percent level.

Table 5-2. Average Hours Worked per Month, by Length of Follow-Up: Ex-Addict Sample

Month After Enrollment in the Sample	Experimental Group Mean	Control Group Mean	Experimental-Control Differential	Mean Hours in Supported Work[a]	
				Hours	*As Percent of Total Hours of Experimentals*
1–3	138.4	32.4	106.0†	126.8	91.6
4–6	116.7	46.7	70.0†	98.9	84.7
7–9	97.3	42.9	54.4†	77.1	79.2
10–12	80.2	46.7	33.5†	51.4	64.1
13–15	64.9	51.4	13.5†	21.4	33.0
16–18	50.4	52.3	−1.9	5.5	10.9
19–21	55.1	55.4	−0.3	1.7	3.1
22–24	61.6	60.2	1.4	1.1	1.8
25–27	63.7	58.9	4.8	0.0	0.0
28–30	66.6	56.3	10.3	0.0	0.0
31–33	73.1	51.9	21.2†	0.0	0.0
34–36	70.4	50.0	20.4†	0.0	0.0

Source: See Table 5-1.

Notes: The data presented in the first three columns are regression-adjusted estimates that control for differences of age, sex, race, education, prior work experience, household composition, site, and length of site operation. Averages are calculated for all members of the sample, including those with no employment in the covered period.

a These data are not regression adjusted. No experimentals should have been in the program beyond month 21. The small number indicated as participating after that time reflects either data errors or failures by program operators to terminate individuals on schedule.

†Statistically significant at the 5 percent level.

Table 5-3.   Average Earnings Per Month, by Length of Follow-Up: Ex-Addict Sample

Month After Enrollment in the Sample	Experimental Group Mean	Control Group Mean	Experimental-Control Differential	Mean Earnings from Supported Work[a]	
				Earnings	As Percent of Total Earnings of Experimentals
1-3	$395.31	$122.30	$273.01†	$355.31	89.9
4-6	348.00	184.58	163.42†	284.68	81.8
7-9	306.08	166.99	139.09†	224.83	73.5
10-12	280.71	205.37	75.34†	154.02	54.9
13-15	251.65	211.81	39.84*	66.17	26.3
16-18	215.51	222.22	-6.71	17.27	8.0
19-21	243.78	250.25	-6.47	5.20	2.1
22-24	281.02	270.36	10.66	3.81	1.4
25-27	287.05	259.88	27.17	1.78	0.6
28-30	304.09	237.45	66.64	0.00	0.0
31-33	332.18	221.85	110.33†	0.00	0.0
34-36	318.60	218.76	99.84†	0.00	0.0

Source: See Table 5-1.

Notes: The data presented in the first three columns are regression-adjusted estimates that control for differences of age, sex, race, education, prior work experience, household composition, site, and length of site operation. Averages are calculated for all members of the sample, including those with no employment in the covered period. Dollar amounts reported are gross earnings unadjusted for inflation.

[a] These data are not regression adjusted. No experimentals should have been in the program beyond month 21. The small number indicated as participating after that time reflects either data errors or failures by program operators to terminate individuals on schedule.

†Statistically significant at the 5 percent level.
*Statistically significant at the 10 percent level.

period, were purposely set below market rates. In contrast, the earnings differentials were relatively high during the months 31 to 36, because of the slightly higher average hourly wage rate earned by the experimentals during that period (see Table 5–4).

This pattern of employment effects raises a number of questions, the most important of which is whether the upturn during the last half of the third year is representative of the results that would have been observed had the full sample been followed for as long as 36 months. As was noted in Chapter 3, only one-third of the total sample was followed for as long as 36 months, and this group may differ from the full sample for a number of reasons. Although the follow-up data cannot provide direct information on the behavior of the 18- and 27-month cohorts during the last 9 months of the research period, a more refined analysis of the responses of the different cohorts helps to inform a discussion of this issue. If the 36-month cohort is not representative, the question is how it differed and whether it would be substantially more effective to target the program at distinct subgroups of the ex-addict population. A related question is why there was such a long delay between the time when participants left supported work and when they began to experience its longer term benefits.

In attempting to generalize the estimates of longer term effects, it is useful to consider the pattern of experimental and control behavior for the 3 cohorts: those followed only for 18, those for 27, and those for the full 36 months after enrollment. The number of hours worked per month by experimentals and controls in each of these cohorts is shown in Figure 5–3. During the period when most experimentals were in the program, all three cohorts exhibited large experimental-control differentials, but these dropped to zero at varying points. Significant differentials persisted, however, throughout months 13 to 15, except for the 18-month cohort, where they continued only through months 7 to 9.

No positive employment differentials were observed again until months 22 to 24, when experimentals increased their employment compared to controls. In the subsequent 3-month period, the differential observed for the 27-month cohort increased slightly (from 2 to 4 hours per month), but that for the 36-month cohort increased sharply, to 19 hours per month, as controls' employment tended to stabilize around 50 to 55 hours per month, while experimentals increased their employment to between 65 and 70 hours per month.

The variation in the employment behavior of the ex-addict cohorts is similar to that observed for the other three target groups. Supported work seems to have been most effective with the individuals

Table 5-4.   Average Hourly Wage Rates of Those Employed, per 3-Month Follow-Up Period: Ex-Addict Sample

Month After Enrollment in the Sample	Experimental Group Mean	Control Group Mean	Nonprogram Wage Rates of Experimentals	Program Wage Rates of Experimentals	
				Wage Rate	As Percent of Non-program Wage Rate
1–3	$2.86	$3.77	$3.45	$2.80	81.2
4–6	2.98	3.95	3.56	2.88	80.9
7–9	3.15	3.89	4.02	2.92	72.6
10–12	3.50	4.40	4.40	3.00	68.2
13–15	3.87	4.12	4.25	3.09	72.2
16–18	4.28	4.25	4.42	3.14	71.0
19–21	4.42	4.52	4.47	3.06	68.5
22–24	4.56	4.49	4.58	3.46a	75.6
25–27	4.51	4.41	4.48	—	—
28–30	4.57	4.22	4.57	—	—
31–33	4.54	4.27	4.54	—	—
34–36	4.53	4.38	4.53	—	—

Source: See Table 5-1.
Notes: The data in this table are not regression adjusted. The wage rate figures are calculated by dividing the average earnings in the given period by average hours. Because these differences are based on aggregate data, significance tests were not available.
aThese data are based on very small sample sizes. No experimentals were employed in supported work programs beyond month 24.

Figure 5-3

TREND IN HOURS WORKED PER MONTH BY COHORT: EX-ADDICT SAMPLE

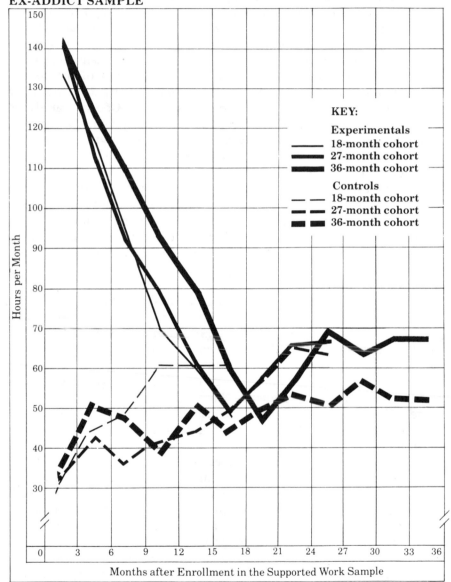

NOTE: To abstract from any changes in sample composition, data in this figure are for individuals who have completed all interviews and for whom there is therefore continuous data covering the periods indicated. An individual belongs to the 18-month cohort (225 people), the 27-month cohort (495 people) or the 36-month cohort (242 people) based on the last follow-up interview he or she received. Data are not regression adjusted.

enrolled in the sample in the early period of the demonstration, and thus followed the longest; however, this difference is not primarily the result of greater employment among the early experimentals, but rather of the relatively low work hours reported by the earlier enrolled controls. Furthermore, only a small part of the cohort differential was found to result from variations in the characteristics of individuals in the subsamples or from their concentration in different sites. This suggests that a large part of the cohort phenomenon probably results from the sharp changes in the labor market over the period of the demonstration. Cohort variations are also not the result of differential participation in government employment programs. Employment in CETA programs was low among both the experimentals and controls, with no significant differences for these groups or across the cohorts.

In conclusion, it is clear that under some conditions—notably those experienced by the 36-month cohort—supported work participation will result in large and significant changes in post-program employment. Under other conditions, however, supported work participation will have a smaller impact. Overall, this suggests that the environment can have a significant effect on the program's outcome.

On the issue of whether the program has had greater impact on particular subsets of the ex-addict group, the supported work data provide only some weak evidence. Moreover, those who benefited most—e.g., individuals with one or more dependents or with little or no recent participation in a job-training program—are not a group that can be legitimately targeted on by changes in eligibility criteria. However, the evidence that the program had larger than average impacts on ex-addicts recently in methadone maintenance programs, and smaller than average impacts on those in drug-free programs, might suggest some refocusing of recruitment policies. Finally, one finding for ex-addicts is consistent with that noted for the other target groups: a common characteristic for the subgroups with relatively more positive impacts is that the controls tended to work less than the average for all target group controls.

There is also relatively little evidence on the reason for the long delay in the timing of the program's employment effects. One possible explanation is that, during the downturn, the experimentals were engaging in a more extensive job search following their departure from the program. For the full ex-addict sample, the data consistently show higher levels of labor force participation and job search activity among experimentals than controls. Another related explanation for the delay in post-program effects may be that a sizable portion of the experimentals received unemployment compensation benefits upon leaving supported work. These individuals thus had less incentive to find alternative employment in the short run and, perhaps, used this period to be more discriminating in looking for it.[2]

Unfortunately, it was not possible to assess clearly the expected impact of supported work under alternative scenarios of unemployment compensation coverage. The estimates of experimental-control differentials during months 16 to 21 would have been positive rather than negative, but the values would have been small and the delays between leaving supported work and significant post-program impacts would still exist. In conclusion, although it is not well understood, the pattern of program impacts shown in Figure 5-2—where the experimental-control differential declines and then, after a delay, recovers—although somewhat sensitive to the unemployment compensation effect, cannot be explained by it.

SUPPORTED WORK'S EFFECTS ON WELFARE AND TOTAL INCOME

Table 5-5 provides information on the sources of income for members of the ex-addict sample. The information on the control group indicates that, in the absence of supported work, about 50 percent of the sample received some welfare payments during the first 9 months after enrollment and over 40 percent in the later periods. During the initial months, when the experimentals were in the program, there was a substantial reduction in the number on welfare (29 percent of the experimentals compared to 51 percent of the controls) and the average welfare benefit ($44 a month for experimentals, including those who did and did not receive benefits, compared to $93 for the controls). During this same period, experimentals were also significantly less likely to receive food stamps. However, these differentials did not persist into the post-program period. In addition, as noted above, significantly more experimentals than controls received unemployment compensation payments in

2. None of the programs enrolling ex-addicts participated in the state unemployment insurance programs. However, as noted in the preceding chapter, experimental group members in some sites gained eligibility for Special Unemployment Assistance (SUA) benefits on the basis of their supported work employment. Among the ex-addict sample, Jersey City was the only site where receipt rates were high and where a sizable experimental-control differential in receipt was observed. Receipt rates and experimental-control differentials in receipt rates were highest among the 36-month cohort and lowest among the 18-month cohort.

Table 5-5. Percent Receiving Income from Various Sources During 9-Month Periods and Average Monthly Income Received: Ex-Addict Sample

Source of Income	Months 1-9		Months 10-18		Months 19-27		Months 28-36	
	Experimental-Control Differential	Control Group Mean	Experimental-Control Differential	Control Group Mean	Experimental-Control Differential	Control Group Mean	Experimental-Control Differential	Control Group Mean
	Percent Receiving							
Earnings	44.8†	50.2	10.8†	53.1	3.5	53.0	10.1*	53.9
Unearned income								
Unemployment compensation	-5.0†	7.4	10.7†	4.3	5.2†	6.0	0.5	7.4
Welfare[a]	-21.7†	50.7	-6.1*	46.7	-0.4	40.2	-3.6	45.1
Food stamps	-10.1†	45.7	-3.5	43.3	1.8	38.8	0.6	42.0
Other[b]	-4.2†	7.1	-2.4*	4.2	-2.1	5.3	2.3	2.2
	Average Monthly Amount[d]							
All sources[c]	$134.09†	$295.50	$36.00	$344.53	$23.17	$373.98	$ 92.03†	$352.40
Earnings	201.44†	159.79	39.20*	220.42	16.42	261.33	101.73†	224.36
Unearned income								
Unemployment compensation	-6.59†	10.86	17.84†	8.42	15.11†	10.31	1.16	16.62
Welfare[a]	-48.49†	92.88	-12.50*	86.99	-3.12	74.70	-9.83	82.84
Food stamp bonus value[e]	-6.01†	20.89	-3.47	22.60	0.37	18.56	0.48	20.90
Other[b]	-4.66	10.24	-2.21	4.61	-3.30	7.86	-0.43	7.14

Source: See Table 5-1.

Notes: All data are regression adjusted.

aWelfare includes AFDC, GA, SSI, and other unspecified cash welfare income.

bOther unearned income includes Social Security, pensions, alimony, and child support.

c"All Sources" includes earned and unearned income, as itemized in the table, and does not include the value of Medicaid or other in-kind benefits.

dAverages are calculated including individuals receiving zero benefits.

eRepresents the difference between the purchase price of the food stamps and their face value.

†Statistically significant at the 5 percent level.

*Statistically significant at the 10 percent level.

months 10 through 27. Finally, as a result of their substantially higher earnings, the experimentals had significantly more total income than did the controls during the first and last 9 months of the study.

SUPPORTED WORK'S EFFECTS ON DRUG USE

Table 5–6, which presents data on the drug use patterns of experimentals and controls, indicates that the supported work program did not have a significant influence on the ex-addicts' use of drugs. For this sample, the most important drug to consider is heroin, which about 20 percent of the experimentals and controls reported having used in the first nine months. The second most widely used drug, other than marijuana or alcohol, was cocaine; about 15 to 16 percent of both groups reported using cocaine. The use of marijuana was widespread among both experimentals and controls and persisted at high levels throughout the study. Keeping these unimpressive results in mind, the program did seem to have an impact on certain subgroups within the target population. It led to reduced prevalence of heroin use among those over 35 years old, among whites and Hispanics, and among short-term heroin users, particularly during the first 18 months.

In general, these subgroup differences with regard to the use of heroin seem to follow a pattern that indicates that the program may have had some effects in reducing heroin when the risks of recidivism were particularly high—that is, where a high percentage of the control group reported heroin use. Where the control group reported a lower percentage of drug use, the program seemed to be ineffective.

Finally, an examination of the use of drugs by employed and unemployed experimentals and controls provides no clear indication that employment and drug use are incompatible. The unemployed members of the sample show only a slightly higher use of drugs than those employed, and in the final 9 months of the study this finding is actually reversed. In addition, there are no convincing experimental-control differences when the unemployed and employed members of the sample are examined separately.

SUPPORTED WORK'S EFFECTS ON CRIMINAL ACTIVITIES

As with drug use, it is difficult to obtain accurate measures of an individual's participation in criminal activities, because people

Table 5-6.   Percent Reporting Drug Use, by Type of Drug and Period of Use: Ex-Addict Sample

Type of Drug	Months 1–9		Months 10–18		Months 19–27		Months 28–36	
	Experimental-Control Differential	Control Group Mean	Experimental-Control Differential	Control Group Mean	Experimental-Control Differential	Control Group Mean	Experimental-Control Differential	Control Group Mean
Any drug (other than marijuana or alcohol)	-2.1	38.2	1.4	32.7	0.5	27.5	2.7	20.7
Heroin								
Any use	-1.3	21.5	-1.0	17.8	1.7	11.7	1.3	8.8
Daily use	n.a.	n.a.	-2.5	7.7	-0.2	4.8	-0.8	4.3
Opiates other than heroin[a]	-0.7	10.1	1.8	5.5	0.9	5.2	-2.4	7.4
Cocaine[a]	2.6	16.2	2.6	15.3	1.5	15.2	-1.4	13.7
Amphetamines, barbiturates, psychedelics, or illegal methadone[a]	0.2	9.2	1.0	9.2	0.3	8.5	-1.7	6.6
Marijuana								
Any use	-0.2	65.4	-0.5	66.3	2.2	62.5	0.8	61.8
Daily use	n.a.	n.a.	-1.4	25.4	-0.2	23.4	2.0	20.7
Alcohol (daily use)	-4.1*	15.7	4.7†	12.1	4.4*	13.3	3.4	13.1

Source: See Table 5-1.

[a]Daily use of other opiates or cocaine or amphetamines, barbiturates, psychedelics, and illegal methadone was reported by less than 5 percent of the ex-addict sample and so is not included in this table.

†Statistically significant at the 5 percent level.

*Statistically significant at the 10 percent level.

n.a. = not available.

engaged in such behavior have an incentive to hide their actions. In the supported work study, both experimentals and controls were asked during periodic interviews about their criminal activity— about the commission of crimes, receipt of illegal income, and about arrests, convictions, and incarcerations. The analysis of these data and other studies on ex-offenders has indicated that the self-reports of actual participation in crimes and illegal income frequently contained either gross exaggerations or severe underreporting. As a result, this document contains only reports on results with regard to the criminal justice system, indicators that could be verified by cross-checks with official records. In order to investigate the accuracy of these self-reported data, a special study was conducted using data from official arrest records and supported work interviews for a sample of ex-addicts and ex-offenders (experimentals and controls) in two states. The comparison of the data from these two sources indicated that both experimentals and controls substantially underreported their arrests: the number of arrests from the official records was about 90 percent higher than the number reported in the interviews. However, and most importantly for the supported work evaluation, there was no significant difference in the extent of underreporting of arrests between the experimental and control groups. Thus, the self-reported data provide a reliable indication of the extent of the difference in arrests between the two groups.[3]

Table 5-7 summarizes the information on the arrests, convictions, and incarcerations of the ex-addict experimentals and controls for each 9-month period of the study. It indicates that supported work had a strong effect on the criminal activity of this target group. In every time period, fewer experimentals than controls were arrested; the effects were particularly strong in months 10 through 18, when two-thirds or more of the experimentals had left the program (see Table 5-1). Likewise, fewer experimentals than controls were convicted or incarcerated, and these differences were also significant for the 10-to-18-month period.

Because of the prevalence and destructiveness of robberies, and because robberies figure prominently in the benefit-cost calculations, these data are reported separately in Table 5-7. Given the nature of the target population, drug-related arrests are also indicated.[4]

---

3. In conducting the cost-benefit analysis summarized in Chapter 8, the estimates of the experimental-control differentials in arrests obtained from the interviews were adjusted to account for this underreporting and for the fact that many crimes do not result in arrests.

4. Arrests are defined by the most serious charge involved, ranked as follows: murder and felonious assault; robbery; burglary; larceny; drug law violations, and other crimes.

Table 5-7.   Arrests, by Type of Offense, Conviction, and Incarceration, during 9-Month Periods: Ex-Addict Sample

Item	Months 1-9		Months 10-18		Months 19-27		Months 28-36	
	Experimental-Control Differential	Control Group Mean	Experimental-Control Differential	Control Group Mean	Experimental-Control Differential	Control Group Mean	Experimental-Control Differential	Control Group Mean
Percent with any arrest	-2.5	19.5	-5.9†	18.6	-2.3	18.2	-5.0	13.5
No. arrests	0.00	0.23	-0.09	0.23	-0.04	0.22	-0.04	0.15
Percent with robbery arrests[a]	-3.4†	4.5	-2.0†	3.3	0.5	2.2	-0.9	1.9
No. robbery arrests	-0.04†	0.05	-0.02†	0.03	0.01	0.02	-0.01	0.02
Percent with drug-related arrests[a]	-1.4	3.6	-3.0†	4.1	-2.4*	4.9	-2.2	3.5
Percent convicted[a]	-0.2	8.7	-3.4*	9.6	-1.6	8.0	-3.4	6.5
Percent incarcerated[a]	0.3	10.3	-4.9†	16.2	-2.9	18.6	-5.9	21.2
No. weeks incarcerated	-0.20	1.81	-1.40†	2.90	-0.66	4.14	-1.20	4.36

Source: See Table 5-1.

Notes: The data presented are regression-adjusted estimates that control for differences of age, sex, race, education, prior work experience, household composition, site, and length of site operation. The data in all cases apply to the entire sample. Average numbers thus include zero values.

aPercentages refer to the entire sample, not just those with any arrest.

†Statistically significant at the 5 percent level.

*Statistically significant at the 10 percent level.

Supported work participation resulted in particularly large reductions in both types of arrest in most periods of the study, with significant changes in robbery arrests in the first two time periods and in drug-related arrests in months 10 to 18, and 19 through 27.

Thus, the program seemed to have been particularly effective during the early period of follow-up when program impacts on earnings were substantial, in reducing those types of arrests that may have economic motivations. Given that the data suggest no significant effects on drug use, it may be therefore that through employment the program provided income that eased the economic pressure to commit crimes in order to continue drug use. However, the crime impacts are not limited to the periods of largest employment impacts, but are particularly impressive in months 10 through 18, when over two-thirds of the experimentals have already left the program (see Table 5-1), and the impacts persist into the post-program period.

Although the crime impacts are spread across most subgroups of the sample, one distinction is of particular interest, given the literature on the behavior of ex-addicts. There is a common belief among correctional authorities that older addicts and offenders tend to "burn out" as they age—that they are prepared to turn to more conventional lives if given the opportunity. The data on criminal activity for the supported work ex-addict group tends to be consistent with this hypothesis. In general, the arrest rates for those over 35 years old were less than the average, and in every period supported work's impacts on arrests were greatest for those over 35 years old, although the differences were not statistically significant. This is a case where the program seemed to have had relatively greater effects on a group for whom the risk of recidivism was lower than average.

Because the separate examination of each 9 months in Table 5-7 may obscure patterns that cumulate over longer periods, Table 5-8 provides data on behavior over different intervals.[5] It indicates that the cumulative effect of supported work was substantial. At the end of 27 months, 43 percent of the controls had been arrested at some time during the period, whereas only 32 percent of the experimentals had been arrested. By the end of the third year (for the portion of the sample with 36 months of data), there was a 34 percent reduction in the arrest rate for experimentals. As can be seen from the table, similar substantial and significant differences occurred in the numbers of arrests and in convictions and incarcerations.

In breaking down the crime results and the employment results to try to explain their interrelationships, it was found that fewer

Table 5-8.   Cumulative Arrests, by Type of Offense, Conviction, and Incarceration: Ex-Addict Sample

Item	Months 1-18		Months 1-27		Months 1-36	
	Experimental-Control Differential	Control Group Mean	Experimental-Control Differential	Control Group Mean	Experimental-Control Differential	Control Group Mean
Percent with any arrest	-8.2†	33.5	-10.9†	43.3	-18.1†	53.1
No. arrests	-0.08	0.48	-0.19†	0.70	-0.43†	1.01
Percent with robbery arrests[a]	-5.2†	7.5	-6.9†	9.8	-13.2†	13.4
No. robbery arrests	-0.06†	8.2	-0.08†	0.11	-0.14†	0.15
Percent with drug-related arrests[a]	-3.8†	7.9	-4.6†	10.5	-7.2	14.0
Percent convicted[a]	-4.3*	17.8	-5.7*	22.1	-13.6*	32.9
Percent incarcerated[a]	-4.4*	20.2	-8.1†	28.4	-14.1*	36.6
No. weeks incarcerated	-1.5*	5.4	-4.0†	9.7	-7.1*	13.8

Source: Interviews conducted between April 1975 and March 1979 with experimentals and controls at four of the supported work sites. Cumulative data for months 1 through 18 are for the sample of 974 individuals who completed baseline, 9-month, and 18-month interviews. Cumulative data for months 1 through 27 are for the sample of 738 individuals who completed baseline, 9-, 18-, and 27-month interviews. Cumulative data for months 1 through 36 are for the sample of 242 individuals who completed baseline, 9-, 18-, 27-, and 36-month interviews. These data refer to a sample of individuals different from that in Table 5-1

Notes: The data presented are regression-adjusted estimates that control for differences of age, sex, race, education, prior work experience, household composition, site, and length of site operation. The data in all cases apply to the entire sample. Average numbers thus include zero values.

aPercentages refer to the entire sample, not just those with any arrest.
†Statistically significant at the 5 percent level.
*Statistically significant at the 10 percent level.

employed experimentals than employed controls were arrested, and that these differences were significant in months 10 to 18 and 19 to 27. However, there was no difference in the rate of arrests between unemployed experimentals and controls. These results suggest that those ex-addict experimentals who had post-program jobs may have been so influenced by their earlier supported work experiences that they had a stronger commitment to reduce their criminal activity than comparable employed controls whose earlier period of employment had not been supported work.

A similar examination was conducted into the relationship between the results for ex-addicts' drug use and rates of arrest. In general, those who used drugs were more likely to be arrested than those who did not, and the experimental-control difference in arrests was larger among drug users than nonusers. In months 10 to 18 and 19 to 27, there were significantly lower rates of arrest among drug-using experimentals than among drug-using controls. Thus, supported work appears to have reduced the criminal activity of those ex-addicts who continued to use drugs and might otherwise be expected to have a stronger economic motivation to commit crimes. This pattern of results also fits with earlier general findings of supported work being more effective for groups of experimentals among whom the risks were especially high.

CONCLUSION

The results summarized in this chapter indicate that supported work did have an effect on the employment and criminal activities of the ex-addict group, but failed to have an impact on their drug use. Employment increased significantly during the time in which the ex-addicts participated in the program and, for the subset of the sample followed the full 36 months, also in the last months of the study. Employment in supported work also led to a consistent reduction in criminal activities as measured under a number of different indicators and over the period of the study; these were particularly concentrated in the first 18 months and in robbery and drug-related crimes.

In a later chapter dealing with the benefit-cost analysis, these effects on employment and crime are quantified and balanced with data on the costs of supported work. It will show that the rather

---

5. The reader is cautioned that Table 5-8 is based on a sample different from that used in Table 5-7 or elsewhere in this chapter. In order to calculate cumulative arrests, the sample was limited to respondents who had completed all of the intervening interviews for each of the three periods reported in the table.

modest post-program employment effects for the early sample, when combined with the social value of the reduction in crime, considerably outweigh the cost of the program for the ex-addict target group.

※ *Chapter 6*

Findings for the Youth Target Group

Overall, supported work appears to have little impact on the employment, drug use, or criminal activities of the youth target group in the five sites where this research was carried out. Though the experimental group worked more than the control group when experimentals were still in the program, this difference did not continue into the post-program period. Overall, in terms of drug use and crime, there was not even this in-program effect. Looking at selected subgroups of the population, there is modest evidence that supported work works better for those who are most disadvantaged. Experimental-control differences are highest for those groups who are least successful in employment or have the most severe crime and drug problems.[1]

EMPLOYMENT, DRUG USE,
AND CRIMINAL ACTIVITY
OF THE CONTROL GROUP

Figure 6-1 shows that the hours worked by the control group start at a low of 30 hours per month and rise steadily throughout the period of the study to over 80 hours per month in months 31 to 33. Compared to the experience of the controls in the other target groups, the youth controls were working more than the AFDC

---

1. The results of the analysis of the youth target group are presented in full in a forthcoming report by Rebecca Maynard, *The Impact of Supported Work on Young School Dropouts*, MDRC, 1980.

Figure 6-1

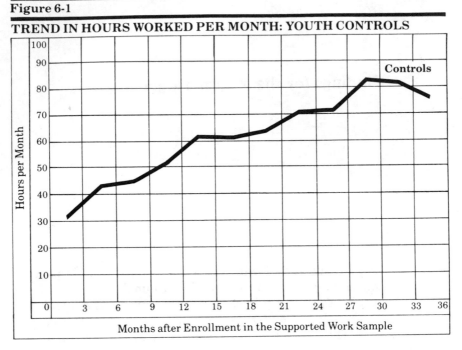

TREND IN HOURS WORKED PER MONTH: YOUTH CONTROLS

Months after Enrollment in the Supported Work Sample

sample at the beginning of the period, about the same number of hours as the ex-addict sample, but fewer hours than the ex-offender sample. However, the upward trend for the youth group over the period of the study is far steeper than for the other three target groups, so that at the end of the period the youth control members were working 40 hours per month more than the AFDC sample, 30 hours more than the ex-addict sample, and 15 hours more than the ex-offender sample (see Figure 4–2).

As with the other target groups, the general upward trend appears to be due to two factors: improvements in the labor market; and the normal process of many people who, unemployed at a given point, get a job at some time in a period of several months—a process referred to earlier as regression to the mean. In the case of the youth group, there is an added factor. It has generally been observed that there is a particularly sharp climb in employment rates for youths between the ages of 16 and 20 years usually attributed to a natural aging process. The youth control group data in the supported work study tend to confirm this experience—with older youths in fact recording a somewhat higher number of work hours.

Another factor that may have contributed to the sharp upward trend of the work hours of the youth control group has been the increasing availability during the study period of new or expanded government programs for youth employment. Thus, whereas CETA-sponsored programs in 1975 served about 1.6 million youths, by 1978 2.3 million youths were enrolled in them. In fact, data for the control group indicate that there was a fairly steady increase over time in the number of youths who held subsidized public sector jobs (from 4 percent in months 1 through 9 to 8 percent in months 28 through 36). Similarly, when regular government jobs are added, the total increased from 9 percent to 21 percent over the same period (see Table 6-4).

Another aspect of employment on which the data shed light is job stability. On the average, there were about two periods of employment for youths during the course of the study—a pattern similar to that of the ex-addicts and ex-offenders. But there is a difference: the average length of the first continuous period of employment of youth controls is about 5 to 5.5 months, whereas for the ex-offenders and the ex-addicts the figure is about 7 months and for the AFDC, 9 months. These figures indicate that youths are less stable in jobs once they get them than the ex-addicts and ex-offenders, and far less stable than AFDC women.

The data also reveal which sections of the control group do better and worse in employment. Youths who entered the survey later in calendar time were more likely to get employment than those who enrolled earlier. Males worked more than females, and those with more prior work experience did better than those with less. Other characteristics, including age, showed only weak relationships to employment.

The percentage of youth controls who were arrested in each of the study periods hovers around 15 percent and shows no particular trend. Over the entire period of the study, as many as 40 percent of the control group reported at least one arrest. About 10 percent of the youth sample reported using drugs other than marijuana and alcohol, and there is also no particular trend in this drug use. About 50 percent of the controls reported marijuana use in the first 9 months, and this percentage increased slightly during the period under study. The main difference between this youth sample and the general youth population appears in heroin usage. The percentage of control youths in supported work who have ever used heroin is twice the national youth average (8 percent versus 4 percent).

SUPPORTED WORK'S EFFECTS
ON EMPLOYMENT

The employment experience of the youth sample is shown in Figure 6-2, which shows work hours of experimentals and controls. The initial substantial difference is due to two sharply contrasting factors: the fact that experimentals had a regular job while in the program; and that the controls had few work hours during the initial period. The difference shrank rapidly as the control group's employment curve began to climb, and as the experimentals dropped out of

Figure 6-2

TREND IN HOURS WORKED PER MONTH: YOUTH SAMPLE

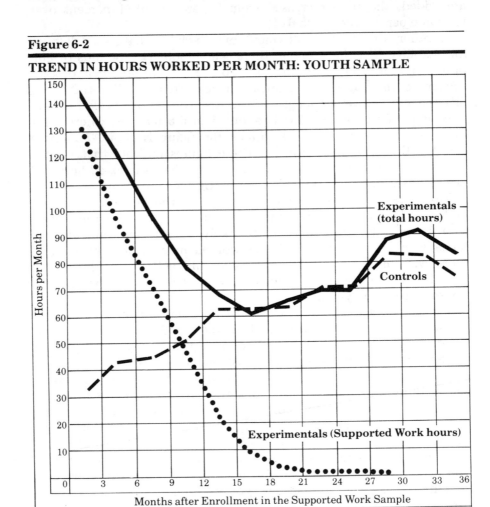

Note: Experimental-control differentials are significant at the 5 percent level for months 1 to 12.

the program. At the end of 15 months, there is no longer any difference between the experimentals and the controls in hours worked. This condition continued through month 30. (After month 30 the work hours of the controls appear to decline slightly, whereas the experimentals seemed to increase their time spent at work. However, the data for the period from 27 through 36 months reflect the experience of a very small, probably unrepresentative sample.)

Tables 6–1, 6–2 and 6–3 present data on employment rates, hours of work, and earnings. After month 12, there are no statistically significant differences in these categories between experimentals and controls. The big difference shows up in the initial phase of the program, when the experimentals have supported work jobs, but that is true of the other target groups as well. Later, as has been noted already, from months 18 through 27 the experimentals increased their time at work, but so did the controls, showing no impact by the program.

A question that could be asked is whether the youth group would have benefited from staying in the program longer. In order to shed light on this issue, an attempt was made in the research to determine whether the length of the youths' stay in the supported work program was correlated with their experience in post-program employment. The data show that there was no significant difference in hours worked or earnings for those who stayed longer in the program. For those who had stayed in the program for the maximum allowable time (about 9 percent), the analysis sought to determine whether they might have benefited from a longer period of employment in supported work. It turns out that 40 percent of this group found a job within the first month after leaving supported work. Thus, there is little indication that a longer stay in the supported work program would have enhanced the program's effects.

At this point, it is necessary to explain why the data in the final period of the study do not carry much weight. To begin with, the sample that was followed for months 28 to 36 is small—153 individuals—and more than half were concentrated at one site. The data in Tables 6–2 and 6–3 illustrate some of the problems that tend to arise with such a small sample. In months 28 to 36, there is a positive difference in hours worked, ranging from 4 to 11, but a negative difference in earnings ranging from -$23 to -$44. None of these differentials is statistically significant. The difference in direction implies that the wage rates of the experimentals were below those of the controls. Whatever accounts for this, it is unlikely to be representative of this youth population. Furthermore, the two seemingly contradictory trends emerge only in the 28-to-36-month period for

Table 6-1. Percent Employed per 3-Month Follow-Up Period: Youth Sample

Month After Enrollment in the Sample	Experimental Group Mean	Control Group Mean	Experimental-Control Differential	Mean For	
				Experimentals With Any Supported Work Job[a]	Experimentals With Only Supported Work Jobs[a]
1-3	96.5	28.7	67.8†	93.0[b]	84.7
4-6	81.8	38.9	42.9†	67.6	61.8
7-9	68.2	40.8	27.4†	49.9	44.3
10-12	54.8	36.0	18.8†	32.3	28.8
13-15	51.0	46.7	4.3	19.8	15.3
16-18	45.1	47.2	-2.1	8.2	5.5
19-21	45.2	42.4	2.8	1.7	1.7
22-24	47.0	49.1	-2.1	1.2	1.2
25-27	51.3	51.0	0.3	0.8	0.4
28-30	51.0	48.5	2.5	0.0	0.0
31-33	59.5	54.7	4.8	0.0	0.0
34-36	57.5	49.9	7.5	0.0	0.0

Source: Interviews conducted between May 1975 and March 1979 with experimentals and controls at five of the supported work sites. The first 18 months of data are for the sample of 861 individuals who completed the baseline, 9- and 18-month interviews; the data on months 19 through 27 are from the 506 individuals who completed 27-month interviews; the data on months 28 through 36 are from the 155 individuals who completed 36-month interviews.

Notes: The data presented in the first three columns are regression-adjusted estimates that control for differences of age, sex, race, education, prior work experience, household composition, site, and length of site operation.

aThese data are not regression adjusted. No experimentals should have been in the program beyond month 21. The small number indicated as participating after that time reflects either data errors or failures by program operators to terminate individuals on schedule.

b2.7 percent of the experimentals never showed up for their supported work jobs, and another 5.7 percent were in the program for less than 30 days. Because employment intervals of less than two weeks were not recorded in interviews, the percentages of this table may actually slightly understate program participation.

†Statistically significant at the 5 percent level.

Table 6-2. Average Hours Worked per Month, by Length of Follow-Up: Youth Sample

Month After Enrollment in the Sample	Experimental Group Mean	Control Group Mean	Experimental-Control Differential	Mean Hours in Supported Work[a]	
				Hours	As Percent of Total Hours of Experimentals
1–3	143.3	31.2	112.1†	131.1	91.5
4–6	120.1	43.9	76.2†	96.2	80.1
7–9	97.1	44.8	52.3†	70.5	72.6
10–12	79.4	50.2	29.2†	46.2	58.2
13–15	67.2	62.2	5.0	21.4	31.9
16–18	60.4	61.3	-0.9	8.8	14.6
19–21	64.4	63.6	0.8	2.4	3.8
22–24	69.6	70.0	-0.4	2.0	2.9
25–27	69.1	70.4	-1.3	0.6	0.9
28–30	87.2	83.0	4.2	0.0	0.0
31–33	92.8	82.2	10.6	0.0	0.0
34–36	83.3	75.8	7.5	0.0	0.0

Source: See Table 6-1.

Notes: The data presented in the first three columns are regression-adjusted estimates that control for differences of age, sex, race, education, prior work experience, household composition, site, and length of site operation. Averages are calculated for all members of the sample, including those with no employment in the covered period.

aThese data are not regression adjusted. No experimentals should have been in the program beyond month 21. The small number indicated as participating after that time reflects either data errors or failures by program operators to terminate individuals on schedule.

†Statistically significant at the 5 percent level.

Table 6-3.   Average Earnings per Month, by Length of Follow-Up: Youth Sample

Month After Enrollment in the Sample	Experimental Group Mean	Control Group Mean	Experimental-Control Differential	Mean Earnings From Supported Work[a]	
				Earnings	As Percent of Total Earnings of Experimentals
1-3	$389.52	$100.15	$289.37†	$353.90	90.9
4-6	340.76	140.51	200.25†	266.80	78.3
7-9	284.40	138.24	146.16†	197.20	69.3
10-12	255.24	163.51	91.73†	134.10	52.5
13-15	218.79	211.16	7.63	63.33	28.9
16-18	208.78	213.04	-4.26	28.23	13.5
19-21	246.22	220.85	25.37	9.33	3.8
22-24	270.77	256.01	14.76	7.75	2.9
25-27	265.98	268.05	-2.07	1.63	0.6
28-30	300.95	323.53	-22.58	0.00	0.0
31-33	323.60	347.73	-24.13	0.00	0.0
34-36	287.13	331.59	-44.46	0.00	0.0

Source: See Table 6-1.

Notes: The data presented in the first three columns are regression-adjusted estimates that control for differences of age, sex, race, education, prior work experience, household composition, site, and length of site operation. Averages are calculated for all members of the sample, including those with no employment in the covered period. Dollar amounts reported are gross earnings unadjusted for inflation.

[a]These data are not regression adjusted. No experimentals should have been in the program beyond month 21. The small number indicated as participating after that time reflects either data errors or failures by program operators to terminate individuals on schedule.

†Statistically significant at the 5 percent level.

this sample. Data produced by these same 154 individuals in months 19 through 27 show a statistically insignificant difference in hours and earnings for that period.

In the case of the AFDC and ex-addict target groups, uneven payments of unemployment compensation appeared to have reduced the employment differentials between experimentals and controls in some periods. In the case of the youth group, unemployment compensation payments to both experimentals and controls were considerably lower than they were for the AFDC and ex-addict groups. About 4 percent of the controls received unemployment compensation in each of the three time periods through month 27. In months 10 through 18, 10 percent of the experimentals received unemployment compensation; in months 19 through 27, 7 percent did so. Thus, there was an experimental-control difference, and it was significant throughout. But analysis indicates that these differentials in unemployment compensation did not have a major impact on the experimental-control differences in key employment indicators.

As to the significance of CETA or WIN jobs in the employment experience of the youth group, Table 6-4 shows, as noted earlier, that they are a factor in the increase in employment and earnings figures. However, even though the differences between experimentals and controls in access to CETA and WIN jobs are not large, experimentals—and especially those who were interviewed 36 months after enrollment—are much less likely than controls to be employed in the public sector. Given the problem that youths have in distinguishing between government jobs and CETA jobs, Table 6-4 suggests that subsidized employment may be providing an important explanation for the employment of the control group.

Because of the absence of significant supported work effects in the post-program period of employment of the youth group as a whole, the study attempted to seek out possible impacts on some subgroups of the target group. The results show at best some suggestions that the program may be more successful with youths under 19 years of age, those raised in intact families, those who have one or more dependents, and those who have had particularly limited work experience. The estimates of the experimental-control differentials for these subgroups are consistently positive and larger than for the overall sample, but only rarely are they statistically significant. As has been noted with other target groups, the larger impact of the program on some subgroups of experimentals seems to reflect the fact that the similar control group had relatively less employment success.

Though not directly related to the question of employment and

Table 6-4. CETA, WIN, and Public Sector Employment During 9-Month Periods: Youth Sample

Item	Months 1-9		Months 10-18		Months 19-27		Months 28-36	
	Experimental Group	Control Group	Experimental Group	Control Group	Experimental Group	Control Group	Experimental Group	Control Group
Percent with CETA or WIN jobs	1.5	3.8	4.4	3.8	6.3	4.9	6.7	7.9
Average monthly earnings from CETA or WIN jobs	$3.34	$7.57	$11.86	$8.56	$19.34	$15.63	$21.74	$55.70
Percent with CETA, WIN, or government jobs	4.2	8.8	11.1	14.0	13.1	11.9	9.3	21.1
Average monthly earnings from CETA, WIN, or government jobs	$8.30	$17.36	$38.24	$38.25	$51.99	$39.54	$37.18	$120.03

Source: See Table 6-1.

Notes: The data in this table are simple subgroup means and are not regression adjusted. No tests of statistical significance were computed. To categorize a job, respondents were asked whether or not a specific job was for state or local government, and whether or not it was part of a special government employment program such as CETA or WIN.

earnings, the amount of education that a youth acquires often determines his potential for future labor market success. A comparison of the rates of participation in educational programs of supported work experimentals and controls revealed that the program did not affect the propensity of the youth group (all of whom were high school dropouts) to return to school or to a General Education (GED) program. Over the 36 months of follow-up, in each 9-month period, between 5 and 16 percent of both experimentals and controls participated in educational programs, the majority at the high school level, but there were no significant differences between the two groups.

SUPPORTED WORK'S EFFECTS ON TOTAL INCOME

Information on the total income of the youth group and the sources of that income is provided in Table 6-5. The lower half of the table shows a clear upward trend in the average monthly income of controls and experimentals. After the first 9 months, when supported work earnings significantly increase the total earnings of experimentals, there are no statistically significant differences in the total income between the two groups. Furthermore, welfare payments to controls rise only from 17 to 21 percent of the sample during the first two years of the study.

In months 1 to 9, and months 10 to 18, there is a small, but statistically significant, difference in welfare payments received by experimentals and controls. During months 1 to 9, this is clearly related to supported work earnings. In months 10 to 18, the lower welfare payments of the experimentals are compensated for by higher unemployment compensation, and in months 19 to 27, there is still a $10 per month differential in unemployment compensation, which is statistically significant. This does not seem to be a disincentive to employment for the youth group. Differentials in earnings for the youths are similar to those for total income, since other sources of unearned income, principally transfer payments, are of relatively little direct importance to this group.

SUPPORTED WORK'S EFFECTS ON DRUG USE

Compared to a national youth sample, a higher percentage of supported work youths reported having used heroin, and a lower percentage, cocaine. The use of marijuana reported by 61 percent of

Table 6-5. Percent Receiving Income from Various Sources During 9-Month Periods and Average Monthly Income Received: Youth Sample

Source of Income	Months 1-9		Months 10-18		Months 19-27		Months 28-36	
	Experimental-Control Differential	Control Group Mean	Experimental-Control Differential	Control Group Mean	Experimental-Control Differential	Control Group Mean	Experimental-Control Differential	Control Group Mean
	Percent Receiving							
Earnings	45.6†	52.5	6.2*	62.7	0.0	62.6	8.7	66.2
Unearned income								
Unemployment compensation	-2.0	4.0	6.8†	3.7	3.8*	3.8	-5.6	6.8
Welfarea	-6.8†	17.0	-3.5	21.4	-1.3	20.6	-11.4*	25.0
Food stamps	-0.5	32.4	-3.7	30.5	-0.6	29.0	6.6	30.3
Otherb	-2.0	6.3	-1.1	5.1	0.4	3.1	0.7	1.7
	*Average Monthly Amount*d							
All sourcesc	$215.01†	$176.04	$21.95	$265.44	$26.99	$311.68	$-54.54	$408.01
Earnings	226.73†	123.95	30.71	205.25	19.30	248.98	-41.53	342.58
Unearned income								
Unemployment compensation	-2.99	5.63	11.16†	4.71	10.14†	5.80	-8.16	10.25
Welfarea	-9.66†	22.85	-12.49†	33.00	-6.20	37.30	-15.75	36.01
Food stamp bonus valuee	0.88	17.52	-3.63*	15.44	-1.42	16.82	5.18	18.78
Otherb	0.94	5.65	-3.34	6.81	5.91	2.42	5.33	0.58

Source: See Table 6-1.

Notes: All data are regression adjusted.

aWelfare includes AFDC, GA, SSI, and other unspecified cash welfare income.

bOther unearned income includes Social Security, pensions, alimony, and child support.

c"All Sources" includes earned and unearned income, as itemized in the table, and does not include the value of Medicaid or other in-kind benefits.

dAverages are calculated including individuals receiving zero benefits.

eRepresents the difference between the purchase price of the food stamps and their face value.

†Statistically significant at the 5 percent level.

*Statistically significant at the 10 percent level.

the supported work sample at the time of enrollment was at about the average for the national sample. Table 6-6 provides data on drug use by experimentals and controls. Heroin use declined somewhat, but the use of cocaine remained fairly constant throughout the first 27 months for both experimentals and controls.

It is clear from the data in Table 6-6 that supported work had no significant effects on drug use among the youth sample in any period. Given this overall lack of significant program effects, further analysis sought again to determine possible impacts on subgroups, but turned out negative. Furthermore, as with the ex-addict and ex-offender groups, no relationship was observed between the amount of drug use and employment, which suggests a greater independence between drug use and employment than is often assumed to exist.

SUPPORTED WORK'S EFFECTS ON CRIMINAL ACTIVITY

On the whole, supported work did not have a significant impact on the criminal behavior of the youth group—either during the program jobs or subsequently, as can be seen in Table 6-7. During each of the first two 9-month periods following enrollment, about 16 percent of both experimentals and controls reported having been arrested at least once, and among those arrested, the average number of arrests was 1.2. Between 15 and 20 percent of the arrests were for robbery, and less than 10 percent for drug-related offenses. There was a sizable percentage of convictions and prison sentences, but at least some of the acts that led to these dispositions may have been committed before the program got in touch with these individuals. However, the overall finding remains: a relatively constant level of convictions and incarcerations and no statistically significant experimental-control differences.

It is conceivable that small, statistically insignificant differences in each of the 9-month periods might develop to the point of statistical significance when the sample is observed for a longer period. Therefore, Table 6-8 presents data on cumulative arrests and convictions. As indicated in the previous chapter, the sample that is the subject of Table 6-8 is slightly different from that of Table 6-7 because, in order to determine cumulative arrests or convictions, it is necessary that the individual not have missed any interview during the entire period. In the case of those for whom 18 months of data are available, 27 percent of the control group had at least one arrest during that period, 16 percent were convicted and 18 percent were

Table 6-6.   Percent Reporting Drug Use, by Type of Drug and Period of Use: Youth Sample

Type of Drug	Months 1-9		Months 10-18		Months 19-27		Months 28-36	
	Experimental-Control Differential	Control Group Mean	Experimental-Control Differential	Control Group Mean	Experimental-Control Differential	Control Group Mean	Experimental-Control Differential	Control Group Mean
Any drug (other than marijuana or alcohol)	-2.9	14.2	0.3	10.2	0.4	10.6	5.8	11.0
Heroin[a]	0.4	3.6	-0.7	2.4	0.6	1.2	0.9	1.0
Cocaine[a]	-1.1	8.2	-1.2	8.2	-1.0	8.4	5.7	9.7
Marijuana								
Any use	4.5	52.4	1.6	51.2	0.3	57.6	0.1	64.1
Daily use	n.a.	n.a.	0.0	22.4	5.4	21.1	-0.3	29.4
Alcohol (daily use)	2.6*	5.5	1.9	9.3	0.7	9.9	-1.6	8.9

Source: See Table 6-1.

[a] Daily use of heroin or cocaine, and any use of other opiates, amphetamines, barbiturates, and psychedelics, was reported by less than 1 percent of the youth sample and so is not included in this table.

*Statistically significant at the 10 percent level.

n.a. = not available.

Table 6-7. Arrests, by Type of Offense, Conviction, and Incarceration, during 9-Month Periods: Youth Sample

Item	Months 1-9		Months 10-18		Months 19-27		Months 28-36	
	Experimental-Control Differential	*Control Group Mean*	*Experimental-Control Differential*	*Control Group Mean*	*Experimental-Control Differential*	*Control Group Mean*	*Experimental-Control Differential*	*Control Group Mean*
Percent with any arrest	0.3	16.8	1.6	15.2	-3.2	13.6	6.4	16.7
No. arrests	0.06	0.20	0.03	0.18	-0.05	0.16	0.09	0.18
Percent with robbery arrests[a]	-0.3	3.4	0.6	2.6	-1.0	3.1	2.2	2.3
No. robbery arrests	-0.00	0.04	0.00	0.03	-0.01	0.04	0.02	0.02
Percent with drug-related arrests[a]	1.0	0.9	-0.5	1.2	0.8	0.4	1.6	1.3
Percent convicted[a]	1.2	9.1	0.0	8.3	-2.3	6.7	-1.8	9.8
Percent incarcerated[a]	-2.7	11.6	2.0	12.6	3.8	15.5	2.5	17.2
No. weeks incarcerated	-0.58	1.62	0.14	2.37	-1.06	3.66	-1.12	3.67

Source: See Table 6-1.

Notes: The data presented are regression-adjusted estimates that control for differences of sex, race, education, prior work experience, household composition, site, and length of site operation. The data in all cases apply to the entire sample. Average numbers thus include zero values.

[a]Percentages refer to the entire sample, not just those with any arrest.

Table 6-8. Cumulative Arrests by Type of Offense, Conviction, and Incarceration: Youth Sample

Item	Months 1-18		Months 1-27	
	Experimental-Control Differential	Control Group Mean	Experimental-Control Differential	Control Group Mean
Percent with any arrest	-0.3	27.0	-8.8*	39.3
No. arrests	0.07	0.38	0.01	0.62
Percent with robbery arrests[a]	0.4	6.1	-3.1	13.0
No. robbery arrests	0.00	0.07	-0.03	0.15
Percent with drug-related arrests[a]	-0.1	2.1	0.9	4.9
Percent convicted[a]	0.5	16.0	-4.0	23.6
Percent incarcerated[a]	-0.6	18.3	-10.2†	28.0
No. weeks incarcerated	-0.7	4.1	-4.8†	10.2

Source: Interviews conducted between May 1975 and March 1979 with experimentals and controls at five of the supported work sites. Cumulative data for months 1 through 18 are for the sample of 861 individuals who completed baseline, 9- and 18-month interviews. Cumulative data for months 1 through 27 are for the sample of 419 individuals who completed baseline 9-, 18-, and 27-month interviews. These data thus refer to a sample of individuals different from that in Table 6-1.

Notes: Results for the 1- to 36-month period are not presented because of the limited sample size. The data presented are regression-adjusted estimates that control for differences of age, sex, race, education, prior work experience, household composition, site, and length of site operation.

aPercentages refer to the entire sample, not just those with any arrest.

†Statistically significant at the 5 percent level.

*Statistically significant at the 10 percent level.

incarcerated—for an average number of four weeks of incarceration. The experimental-control differentials are not statistically significant.

Among those for whom 27 months of follow-up data are available, the results are somewhat more favorable: only 30 percent of the experimentals as compared with 38 percent of the controls had been arrested during the 27 months following enrollment. Similarly, experimentals among this group reported a significantly lower rate and average duration of incarceration over this full period. Much of this more favorable pattern of effects appears to be attributable to a consistently more positive response to supported work among those earlier enrollees who were followed beyond month 18, compared with the later enrollees. However, the lack of similar findings for the smaller sample followed for 36 months suggests caution in reaching a conclusion on this issue.

Further analysis of the data on those for whom we have 27-month data yielded a significant finding: program effects occurred in those subgroups where the controls were arrested more often during the 27-month period. This is consistent with other findings that supported work is most effective where the risks of difficulties with crime, drugs, or employment are unusually high. With respect to arrests, the groups with high rates of arrest, for which some program effect was indicated, included: youths younger than 19 years, those with 9 or more years of education, and youths who had some work experience before entering the program. When these findings are correlated with those from the employment analysis, the results are equivocal. For youths younger than 19 years of age, there is also some indication of greater program success. However, for the other subgroups, there is little correspondence between the crime and employment effects.

CONCLUSIONS

Supported work had little effect on the employment of members of the youth group beyond the period in which they participated in the program, and no noticeable effect on drug use. There is some indication that the program led to a reduction in criminal activities, although there is no clear or consistent pattern. The youths stayed in the program an average of about 7 months. In one sense, this could be viewed as a program success, for this is more than 1 month longer than the control group members stayed in their first jobs. Furthermore, it must be remembered that the controls' length of stay on the job applies to only that portion of the group who are employed, whereas the length of stay for the experimentals applies to the entire group. Thus, there is some suggestion that the youths do stay in supported work somewhat longer than they could be expected to stay in a nonprogram job.

Focusing solely on the experimental-control differentials can obscure one of the most important facts that emerges from the research on the youth group, notably the sharp rise in the relatively high level of employment among the control group. At some time during the period of the study, 80 to 90 percent of the controls were employed. This far exceeds the rate for any of the other target groups, and suggests that the program may not have been tightly enough focused on the most disadvantaged youth group. This conclusion would be consistent with the general finding that the program appears to be most effective when the individual is most unsuccessful with employment or has serious drug or crime problems. However, at this stage, it is not apparent how better to identify the youths most likely to benefit from the program.

The recent growth in federally sponsored programs attempting to deal with youth employment problems suggests that there is strong social concern for this group. There is some evidence that the youths stay in supported work longer than they would on a regular job. But consideration of using the supported work mechanism for keeping youths at work should go hand in hand with calculating the costs. Even though some information on this question is provided in the chapter on program benefits and costs, the absence of comparable data on the experience of youths in alternative employment and training programs makes it difficult to determine whether supported work is cost effective for this target group.

❋ *Chapter 7*

Findings for the Ex-Offender Target Group

This chapter summarizes the impact of the supported work program on members of the ex-offender target group.[1]

It draws on information collected in interviews with experimentals and controls over a 36-month period at seven of the local sites. The findings suggest that supported work had only limited impact on this group. While participants were in the program they worked more and were less dependent on welfare programs, but overall there was no reduction in crime or drug use. Moreover, in the post-program period the employment impacts declined sharply to the point where they became statistically insignificant. There are some indications of possible long-term impacts on employment behavior, crime, and drug use for the early enrollees in the sample, but they are not conclusive.

The first section of this chapter briefly reviews the activities of the control group over the 36 months in order to clarify the expected behavior of this target group in the absence of the program. The subsequent sections contrast the data for experimentals and controls and discuss the changes that resulted from participation in supported work.

1. The results of the analysis of the ex-offender target group are presented in full in a forthcoming report by Irving Piliavin and Rosemary Gartner, *The Impact of Supported Work on Ex-Offenders*, MDRC, 1980.

EMPLOYMENT, DRUG USE, AND CRIMINAL ACTIVITIES OF THE CONTROL GROUP

As with the previously discussed target groups, Figure 7-1 shows that employment for controls rose gradually over time. During the first 6 months after random assignment, the control group substantially increased the average number of hours worked until it reached about 50 hours per month. Thereafter, employment continued to grow, though at a much slower rate. Thus, by the final 3-month period, almost 3 years after the baseline interview, ex-offender controls were working nearly 65 hours per month. As with the other target groups, this increase in controls' employment was the result of two factors. Initially, during months 1 to 9, this was almost entirely due to the phenomenon previously labeled regression to the mean, whereas later increases were the product of this factor and improved local labor market conditions.

Compared to the other target groups, the ex-offender controls initially showed the most favorable employment experience. During

Figure 7-1

TREND IN HOURS WORKED PER MONTH: EX-OFFENDER CONTROLS

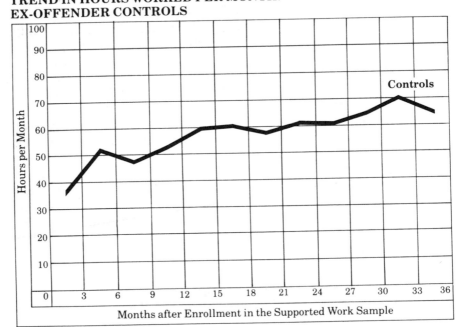

the first year after enrollment in the sample, ex-offender controls worked more hours than any of the other target groups. After month 12, however, the youth controls assumed first place and the ex-offenders dropped to second. Comparisons among the target groups further reveal that, if adjustments are made for differential rates of incarceration among the target groups, the unincarcerated youths and ex-offenders behave similarly and work much more than either ex-addicts or AFDC women.

When the three research cohorts (composed of individuals followed for only 18, only 27, and the full 36 months) are examined separately, a pattern emerges similar to that for the ex-addicts. In general, for any given month after random assignment, employment is higher among the individuals who enrolled later (the 18-month cohort) than those who enrolled earlier (the 36-month cohort).

Arrests among the ex-offender controls were particularly high: about 35 percent of the sample reported having been arrested during the first 9 months after enrollment. This figure declined to about 20 percent during months 10 to 18, and remained at that level through month 36. The ex-offender target group had a higher arrest rate than either the ex-addict or youth control samples, for whom the rates were about 18 and 15 percent, respectively. A cumulative arrest rate of 65 percent was recorded for the ex-offender controls during months 1–36, and about an equal number were incarcerated. Between 8 and 21 percent overall were arrested for robbery, and about 7 percent for drug-related offenses.

Drug use was also high, though below that of the ex-addict group. About 35 percent of the sample reported using some drug other than marijuana or alcohol during months 1–9, and between 25 and 30 percent did so thereafter. Heroin usage also declined over time, with about 15 percent reporting some use in months 1–9 and between 8 and 11 percent thereafter.

SUPPORTED WORK'S EFFECTS ON EMPLOYMENT

Figure 7-2 graphs the trend in hours worked per month for the experimental and control groups. As with all the other groups, it shows that supported work had large, positive employment impacts on ex-offender experimentals in the early months after their enrollment in the demonstration. But the impact did not hold up once they left the program. Thus, although experimentals worked over 100 hours per month more than controls during the first 3 months

Figure 7-2

TREND IN HOURS WORKED PER MONTH: EX-OFFENDER SAMPLE

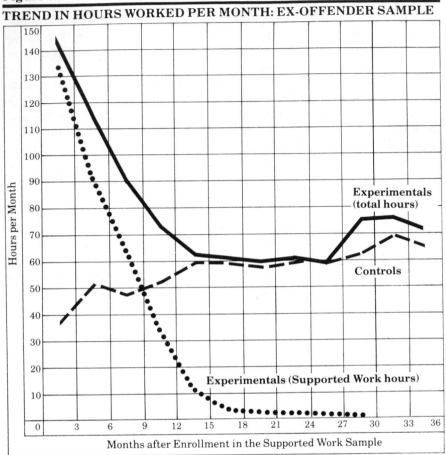

Note: Experimental-control differentials are significant at the 5 percent level for months 1 to 12.

after enrollment, differences between the two groups became insignificant after month 12 and remained negligible until month 27. Although this rapid decay of program impact was in part a reflection of the increase in work hours of the controls, its principal cause was the behavior of the experimentals themselves. Their hours at work declined sharply after the initial months. The ex-offender sample dropped out of the program quickly, spending an average of only 5.9 months in the program, which is less than any other target group. And, once out of the program, the ex-offender experimentals did not work significantly more than the controls.

Thus, during months 15 to 27, when almost no ex-offenders remained in supported work, there was virtually no difference in hours worked between experimentals and controls.

After month 27, however, following a pattern similar to the ex-addict group, some indications of a possible delayed post-program impact emerged, though not as strongly as for the ex-addicts. As indicated in Tables 7-1, 7-2, and 7-3, there are positive though not statistically significant differences between experimentals and controls during months 28 to 36. For example, experimentals earned an average of $56 to $68 a month more than controls did in this period. However, the explanation for this apparent upturn between the last two 9-month periods is not the same as that for the ex-addicts. For that group, the trend reflected both an actual increase in the program's impact on the 36-month cohort which was interviewed during both periods, and a change in the composition of the sample over time. For the ex-offenders, however, only the latter change occurred. Figure 7-3, which graphs the employment of the three subsets of the ex-offender sample, indicates that the group of early enrollees followed through the full 36 months did not experience an increase in program impact during this later period. It would be a mistake, therefore, to view the larger differences in the last follow-up periods as signs of an upturn in program impact. Instead, they reflect the fact that, throughout, the program had a larger impact on the earliest enrollees in the sample.

As can be seen in Table 7-4, experimental-control differences in wage rates contributed to the earnings differentials noted in Table 7-3. During the period when experimentals were participating in supported work, the wage rates of employed experimentals were lower than those of employed controls. This is consistent with supported work policy, which purposefully set program wages below the comparable market wage. The relatively high nonprogram wage rates of experimentals in the first few months probably result from a selective few experimentals leaving supported work because they could command higher wage jobs outside the program. However, in the period when most of the experimentals were no longer in the program, the wages of the employed were between 5 and 60 cents per hour higher for experimentals than for controls. This is why, in the late periods, the difference in earnings is greater than the difference in hours worked.

In two respects, the findings for the ex-offenders run counter to those discovered for the other target groups. First, for the AFDC and ex-addict samples, unemployment compensation appears to have reduced the employment differentials between experimentals

Table 7-1. Percent Employed per 3-Month Follow-Up Period: Ex-Offender Sample

Month After Enrollment in the Sample	Experimental Group Mean	Control Group Mean	Experimental-Control Differential	Mean for Experimentals With Any Supported Work Job[a]	Mean for Experimentals With Only Supported Work Jobs[b]
1-3	93.7	38.0	55.7†	90.7[b]	81.2
4-6	76.3	40.4	35.9†	63.2	56.0
7-9	62.4	39.2	23.2†	43.3	37.8
10-12	51.4	39.3	12.1†	24.7	20.4
13-15	48.2	44.1	4.1	11.8	7.1
16-18	46.0	44.6	1.4	3.8	2.5
19-21	41.8	41.0	0.8	2.0	1.4
22-24	43.9	42.4	1.5	1.2	1.0
25-27	42.7	43.6	-0.9	0.6	0.6
28-30	49.0	44.8	4.2	0.0	0.0
31-33	51.8	47.8	4.0	0.0	0.0
34-36	50.9	45.2	5.7	0.0	0.0

Source: Interviews conducted between April 1975 and March 1979 with experimentals and controls at seven of the supported work sites. The first 18 months of data are for the sample of 1,497 individuals who completed the baseline, 9- and 18-month interviews; the data on months 19 through 27 are from the 995 individuals who completed 27-month interviews; the data on months 28 through 36 are from the 302 individuals who completed 36-month interviews.

Notes: The data presented in the first three columns are regression-adjusted estimates that control for differences of age, sex, race, education, prior work experience, household composition, sites, and length of site operation.

a These data are not regression adjusted. No experimentals should have been in the program beyond month 21. The small number indicated as participating after that time reflects either data errors or failures by program operators to terminate individuals on schedule.

b Of the experimentals, 2.3 percent never showed up for their supported work jobs, and another 7.3 percent were in the program for less than 30 days. Because employment intervals of less than two weeks were not recorded in interviews, the percentages in this table may actually slightly understate program participation.

†Statistically significant at the 5 percent level.

Table 7-2. Average Hours Worked per Month, by Length of Follow-Up: Ex-Offender Sample

Month After Enrollment in the Sample	Experimental Group Mean	Control Group Mean	Experimental-Control Differential	Mean Hours in Supported Work[a]	
				Hours	As Percent of Total Hours of Experimentals
1–3	144.4	37.1	107.7†	133.7	92.3
4–6	113.8	51.0	62.8†	91.0	80.0
7–9	90.9	47.5	43.4†	63.4	69.7
10–12	73.6	52.7	20.9†	34.7	47.1
13–15	63.7	59.4	4.3	12.8	20.1
16–18	60.1	59.5	0.6	3.8	6.3
19–21	59.1	57.9	1.2	2.8	4.7
22–24	60.6	60.8	-0.2	1.4	2.3
25–27	59.8	59.8	0.0	0.6	1.0
28–30	76.1	63.9	12.2	0.0	0.0
31–33	77.5	69.9	7.6	0.0	0.0
34–36	71.8	64.6	7.2	0.0	0.0

Source: See Table 7-1.

Notes: The data presented in the first three columns are regression-adjusted estimates that control for differences of age, sex, race, education, prior work experience, household composition, site, and length of site operation. Averages are calculated for all members of the sample, including those with no employment in the covered period.

[a]These data are not regression adjusted. No experimentals should have been in the program beyond month 21. The small number indicated as participating after that time reflects either data errors or failures by program operators to terminate individuals on schedule.

†Statistically significant at the 5 percent level.

Table 7-3.   Average Earnings per Month, by Length of Follow-Up: Ex-Offender Sample

Month After Enrollment in the Sample	Experimental Group Mean	Control Group Mean	Experimental-Control Differential	Mean Earnings From Supported Work[a] Earnings	As Percent of Total Earnings of Experimentals
1-3	$446.91	$138.74	$308.17†	$383.82	85.9
4-6	385.74	185.15	200.59†	265.53	68.8
7-9	323.94	173.74	150.20†	191.17	59.0
10-12	276.56	221.37	55.19†	107.24	38.8
13-15	274.88	246.15	28.73	40.98	14.9
16-18	269.11	250.10	19.01	13.62	5.1
19-21	265.73	252.92	12.81	11.17	4.2
22-24	273.81	265.63	8.18	6.27	2.3
25-27	266.80	263.72	3.08	2.69	1.0
28-30	353.14	285.48	67.66	0.00	0.0
31-33	375.77	319.99	55.78	0.00	0.0
34-36	361.28	295.35	65.93	0.00	0.0

Source: See Table 7-1.

Notes: The data presented in the first three columns are regression-adjusted estimates that control for differences of age, sex, race, education, prior work experience, household composition, site, and length of site operation. Averages are calculated for all members of the sample, including those with no employment in the covered period. Dollar amounts reported are gross earnings unadjusted for inflation.

aThese data are not regression adjusted. No experimentals should have been in the program beyond month 21. The small number indicated as participating after that time reflects either data errors or failures by program operators to terminate individuals on schedule.

†Statistically significant at the 5 percent level.

Figure 7-3

TREND IN HOURS WORKED PER MONTH BY COHORT: EX-OFFENDER SAMPLE

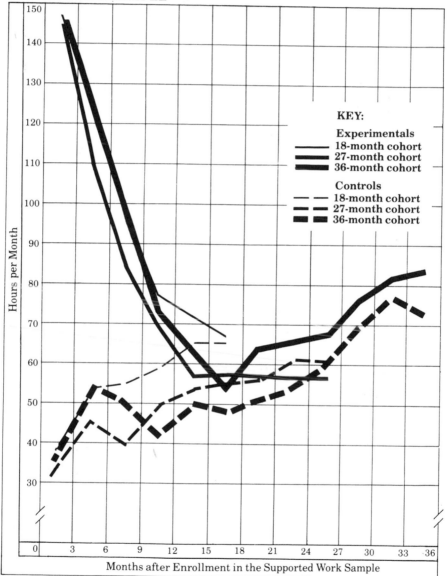

KEY:

Experimentals
—— **18-month cohort**
━━ **27-month cohort**
━━ **36-month cohort**

Controls
– – **18-month cohort**
■ ■ **27-month cohort**
■ ■ **36-month cohort**

Hours per Month

Months after Enrollment in the Supported Work Sample

NOTE: To abstract from any changes in sample composition, data in this figure are for individuals who have completed all interviews and for whom there is therefore continuous data covering the periods indicated. An individual belongs to the 18-month cohort (636 people), the 27-month cohort (609 people), or the 36-month cohort (219 people) based on the last follow-up interview he or she received. Data are not regression-adjusted.

Table 7-4. Average Hourly Wage Rates of Those Employed, by Length of Follow-Up: Ex-Offender Sample

Month After Enrollment in the Sample	Experimental Group Mean	Control Group Mean	Nonprogram Wage Rates of Experimentals	Program Wage Rates of Experimentals	
				Wage Rate	As Percent of Nonprogram Wage Rate
1–3	$3.09	$3.74	$5.68	$2.87	50.5
4–6	2.22	3.63	5.27	2.92	55.4
7–9	3.56	3.66	4.83	3.02	62.5
10–12	3.76	4.20	4.35	3.09	71.0
13–15	4.32	4.14	4.48	3.20	71.4
16–18	4.48	4.20	4.54	3.58	78.9
19–21	4.50	4.37	4.52	3.99	88.3
22–24	4.52	4.37	4.52	4.48[a]	99.1
25–27	4.46	4.41	4.46	4.48[a]	100.5
28–30	4.64	4.47	4.64	—	—
31–33	4.85	4.58	4.85	—	—
34–36	5.17	4.57	5.17	—	—

Source: See Table 7-1.

Notes: The data in this table are not regression adjusted. The wage rate figures are calculated by dividing the average earnings in the given period by average hours. Because these differences are based on aggregate data, significance tests were not available.

[a] These data are based on very small sample sizes. No experimentals were employed in supported work programs beyond month 27.

and controls. For the ex-offenders, this does not seem to be the case: both experimentals and controls received unemployment compensation at relatively low rates. Second, for the ex-offenders, there were no significant positive differences in the employment of subgroups of experimentals and controls from months 19 to 36. Moreover, the small and insignificant differences that could be discerned did not follow the general pattern of the other target groups, where the most disadvantaged benefit the most from supported work.

SUPPORTED WORK'S EFFECTS ON WELFARE AND TOTAL INCOME

Table 7-5 provides a breakdown of the sources of income for the ex-offender sample. About 30 percent of the controls reported receiving welfare payments in each of the 9-month periods. The rate exceeded that of the youths, but fell below those of the ex-addicts and AFDC women. Overall, the trend in welfare receipt is the mirror image of earnings. At the outset, while the experimentals were in the supported work program and earnings' differentials were large, there was a significant drop in the percentage of experimentals receiving welfare and in the average dollar amount received. But welfare payments rose again later on, as experimentals' earnings began to drop and to approach the level of the controls.

In terms of total income, the results follow those for earnings and hours worked. Initially, the difference in total income is quite large, but after month 9, it becomes insignificant. In months 10–18, although the earnings of experimentals and controls differ little from each other, the experimentals still receive significantly less welfare than controls. This is most likely due to normal delays in the process of going on welfare. Although not discussed earlier, this phenomenon is also evident with other target groups.

SUPPORTED WORK'S EFFECTS ON DRUG USE

Table 7-6 presents data on the percentage of experimentals and controls who reported using various categories of drugs. Considering first the use of heroin, the most serious type of illicit drug use, there were no statistically significant program impacts. During each of the four 9-month periods, between 5 and 14 percent of both experimentals and controls reported some use of heroin. Experimental-control

Table 7-5. Percent Receiving Income from Various Sources during 9-Month Periods and Average Monthly Income Received: Ex-Offender Sample

Source of Income	Months 1-9		Months 10-18		Months 19-27		Months 28-36	
	Experimental-Control Differential	Control Group Mean	Experimental-Control Differential	Control Group Mean	Experimental-Control Differential	Control Group Mean	Experimental-Control Differential	Control Group Mean
				Percent Receiving				
Earnings	37.2†	58.7	6.8†	59.2	3.2	53.3	1.2	57.8
Unearned income								
Unemployment compensation	-3.2†	4.8	3.3*	7.4	0.7	6.3	-0.7	7.2
Welfare^a	-12.6†	28.1	-7.6†	29.0	0.4	24.0	-3.1	29.2
Food stamps	-4.4	36.0	-2.9	33.4	-1.0	30.0	-5.9	34.2
Other^b	-1.9	5.6	-3.1†	5.6	-1.4	4.0	0.3	3.1
				Average Monthly Amount^d				
All sources^c	$177.18†	$239.00	$7.47	$341.01	$18.17	$321.00	$78.11	$366.56
Earnings	200.36†	178.38	25.16	260.83	14.99	254.18	62.60	304.20
Unearned income								
Unemployment compensation	-4.64†	5.57	5.31	11.20	3.06	8.58	5.02	10.63
Welfare^a	-17.41†	33.54	-16.10†	44.80	2.39	37.38	-1.44	41.02
Food stamp bonus value^e	-2.68*	15.00	-3.42†	16.10	-0.40	12.50	-0.90	12.53
Other^b	1.36	6.60	-3.55	8.11	-3.38	9.12	-0.21	4.91

Source: See Table 7-1.

Notes: All data are regression adjusted.

aWelfare includes AFDC, GA, SSI, and other unspecified cash welfare income.

bOther unearned income includes Social Security, pensions, alimony, and child support.

cAll sources includes earned and unearned income, as itemized in the table, and does not include the value of Medicaid or other in-kind benefits.

dAverages are calculated including individuals receiving zero benefits.

eRepresents the difference between the purchase price of the food stamps and their face value.

†Statistically significant at the 5 percent level.

*Statistically significant at the 10 percent level.

Table 7-6. Percent Reporting Drug Use, by Type of Drug and Period of Use: Ex-Offender Sample

Type of Drug	Months 1–9		Months 10–18		Months 19–27		Months 28–36	
	Experimental-Control Differential	Control Group Mean	Experimental-Control Differential	Control Group Mean	Experimental-Control Differential	Control Group Mean	Experimental-Control Differential	Control Group Mean
Any drug (other than marijuana or alcohol)	-4.2*	34.2	-3.0	29.0	-1.3	24.1	-11.2†	28.2
Heroin[a]	0.2	14.1	-2.3	10.8	0.0	7.5	-3.8	8.4
Opiates, other than heroin[a]	-0.5	10.5	-2.4*	9.1	-3.1*	9.3	-2.4	5.9
Cocaine[a]	-3.1	21.0	-1.4	18.3	1.3	13.7	-6.6	19.4
Amphetamines, barbiturates, or psychedelics	-1.8	9.7	1.4	5.5	-0.5	6.0	-0.8	3.9
Marijuana								
Any use	-0.8	65.5	-2.2	66.0	-5.0	58.1	-6.8	53.7
Daily use	n.a.	n.a.	-4.9†	26.0	-5.7†	25.3	-7.5	25.3
Alcohol (daily use)	-2.2	14.4	-0.2	15.5	2.9	16.1	1.6	20.5

Source: See Table 7-1.

[a]Daily use of heroin, other opiates, and cocaine was reported by less than 5 percent of the ex-offender sample and so are not included in this table.

†Statistically significant at the 10 percent level.

*Statistically significant at the 5 percent level.

n.a. = not available.

differences were small and did not always favor the experimental group.

The percentage reporting the use of any drug other than marijuana or alcohol presents a somewhat more positive picture. Table 7–6 shows that, in each of the four observation periods, fewer experimentals than controls used heavy drugs. These experimental-control differences, moreover, are statistically significant in both the first and last 9-month periods. Closer analysis reveals, however, that this positive program effect is not characteristic of all the sample but is found primarily among the early enrollees. This is in part a result of a concentration of this subset of the sample in a site where there are relatively large program effects on drug use.

There is also some indication that the program affected the drug use of older experimentals. For the group between 26 and 35 years old, the experimental-control differentials in the use of any drug (other than marijuana or alcohol) are favorable in all four time periods and statistically significant in all but months 10 through 18. This drug effect for the older ex-offenders accords with the findings for the ex-addicts, where significant program effects on heroin use were discovered for those over 35 years of age.

SUPPORTED WORK'S EFFECTS ON CRIMINAL ACTIVITIES

Tables 7–7 and 7–8 provide information on arrests, convictions, and incarcerations reported by ex-offender experimentals and controls. As noted in Chapter 5, a study comparing this self-reported data with official records at two sites indicated that both groups substantially underreported their arrests, but that they did so at similar rates. Thus, the tables understate the actual arrests of both experimentals and controls, but in a manner that is unbiased between the two groups.

The arrest data indicate that supported work has no persistent impact on criminal activities, either while the experimentals are in the program or afterward. None of the cumulative differentials in Table 7–8 are statistically significant, and the only significant finding for a single time period (shown in Table 7–7) occurs during the last 9 months of the study, when there are data only for the subsample followed for the full 36 months. Moreover, a more detailed examination of the program effects for the subsets of the sample with different length of follow-up indicates that throughout the study period the program impacts in crime are larger for the early enrollees. Although this cohort effect is consistent with the

Table 7-7. Arrests, by Type of Offense, Conviction, and Incarceration, during 9-Month Periods: Ex-Offender Sample

Item	Months 1-9		Months 10-18		Months 19-27		Months 28-36	
	Experimental-Control Differential	Control Group Mean	Experimental-Control Differential	Control Group Mean	Experimental-Control Differential	Control Group Mean	Experimental-Control Differential	Control Group Mean
Percent with any arrest	-2.20	34.20	4.10*	23.20	1.80	20.70	-8.70*	22.80
No. arrests	-0.03	0.48	0.04	0.32	0.09	0.26	-0.11*	0.27
Percent with robbery arrests[a]	0.02	5.00	-0.40	3.40	1.00	3.30	-3.30	5.00
No. robbery arrests	0.00	0.05	-0.01	0.04	0.01	0.03	-0.03	0.05
Percent with drug-related arrests[a]	0.42	3.00	-0.46	3.10	0.60	2.30	-0.20	1.20
Percent convicted[a]	-3.1	16.7	3.6*	11.6	1.2	12.3	-4.5	11.4
Percent incarcerated[a]	-1.9	28.7	2.8	27.2	0.2	32.9	-5.1	34.2
No. weeks incarcerated	-0.39	4.52	0.66	6.19	0.30	8.10	-0.46	8.41

Source: See Table 7-1.

Notes: The data presented are regression-adjusted estimates that control for differences of age, sex, race, education, prior work experience, household composition, site, and length of site operation. The data in all cases apply to the entire sample. Average numbers thus include zero values.

[a]Percentages refer to the entire sample, not just those with any arrest.

*Statistically significant at the 10 percent level.

Table 7-8.　Cumulative Arrests, by Type of Offense, Conviction, and Incarceration: Ex-Offender Sample

Item	Months 1-18		Months 1-27		Months 1-36	
	Experimental-Control Differential	Control Group Mean	Experimental-Control Differential	Control Group Mean	Experimental-Control Differential	Control Group Mean
Percent with any arrest	1.00	46.20	0.40	53.30	-8.00	64.75
No. arrests	0.00	0.81	0.03	1.10	-0.50	1.66
Percent with robbery arrests[a]	-0.80	8.10	1.50	10.10	-8.24	21.03
No. robbery arrests	0.00	0.08	0.03	0.12	-0.11	0.26
Percent with drug-related arrests[a]	-0.40	5.90	-0.30	7.50	-2.30	7.70
Percent convicted[a]	-1.0	26.4	-0.2	32.1	8.5	35.4
Percent incarcerated[a]	-1.00	39.10	-1.60	47.00	-13.91	57.50
No. weeks incarcerated	0.28	10.71	0.97	18.97	-1.03	29.86

Source: Interviews conducted between April 1975 and March 1979 with experimentals and controls at seven of the supported work sites. Cumulative data for months 1 through 18 are for the sample of 1,497 individuals who completed baseline, 9- and 18-month interviews. Cumulative data for months 1 through 27 are for the sample of 829 individuals who completed baseline, 9-, 18-, and 27-month interviews. Cumulative data for months 1 through 36 are for the sample of 219 individuals who completed baseline, 9-, 18-, 27-, and 36-month interviews. These data refer to a sample of individuals different from that in Table 7-1.

Notes: The data presented are regression-adjusted estimates that control for differences of age, sex, race, education, prior work experience, household composition, site, and length of site operation. The data in all cases apply to the entire sample. Average numbers thus include zero values.

aPercentages refer to the entire sample, not just those with any arrest.

findings on drug use and employment, the reason for the variation is not clear. Part of the difference results from site effects—that is, the fact that this subsample is concentrated at sites where the program had larger impacts—but the rest remains unexplained. In terms of other subgroups of the sample, an examination of the program's effects on criminal activity does not indicate that the program was effective with any particular group except for a slight suggestion that there was an impact on ex-offenders over the age of 25 years.

CONCLUSIONS

The results summarized in this chapter show that supported work was not effective in increasing the employment or reducing the welfare receipt, drug use, or criminal activities of the ex-offender group over the longer term. While in the program, ex-offenders seemed to benefit from supported work—they worked more hours and earned more dollars than controls—but these results did not persist once they left the program. There were, however, some indications of a program effect on the employment and criminal activities of the early enrollees, and a somewhat stronger effect on the drug use of this group. There was also a hint of program success in terms of drug use and crime on the ex-offenders over 25 years of age. But these differences should be viewed cautiously, because there were not similar findings for the total sample.

The Benefits and Costs of Supported Work

The discussion in the preceding chapters shows that supported work produces a complex pattern of change in the employment, welfare payments, and criminal activities of individuals in the four target groups. It also shows that these effects are purchased at an average public subsidy cost of $5,740 per participant. This chapter presents the summary results of an extensive study that attempted to quantify the outcomes of the program and to compare these figures to program cost, in an effort to answer the question as to whether in economic terms the benefits justify the expense.[1]

Although this approach is useful in providing an overall assessment of supported work's effectiveness, it has limitations and risks. Certain important benefits and costs simply cannot be accurately measured and are therefore not included in the summary estimates. Moreover, this type of analysis calls for assumptions about the value of specific items and for judgments on the longer term extrapolation of benefits and costs that were directly measured only for up to 27 or 36 months. To reduce the risks of this kind of analysis, the research design developed two analytical frameworks: (1) a series of benchmark estimates that contain the researchers' "best guess" on each component of the analysis; and (2) a range of alternative estimates that indicate the sensitivity of the calculation to changes in key assumptions. In this way it is hoped that the reader will both under-

---

1. The more complete results of this analysis are presented in a forthcoming report by Peter Kemper, David Long, and Craig Thornton, *The Supported Work Evaluation: Final Benefit-Cost Analysis*, MDRC, 1980.

stand the perspective presented in the data and the impact of alternative approaches.

Against this background, it is important to note that for three target groups the general trend of the results is remarkably unaffected by reasonable variations in the assumptions. For the AFDC women and ex-addicts, the benefits exceed the costs under all but extreme assumptions. For the youths, the contrary is true. But in the case of the ex-offenders, where the program's impact on employment and crime is unclear, the cost-benefit analysis, too, is inconclusive.

This chapter covers only the highlights of the research methodology and findings. A more detailed presentation will be contained in a forthcoming series of reports on the supported work research effort.

THE BENEFIT-COST METHODOLOGY

The benefits and costs of supported work were analyzed and are presented here from three perspectives: that of society as a whole; that of the supported workers themselves; and that of the rest of society, the nonparticipants, sometimes referred to as the taxpayers. The overall social perspective is the most comprehensive and seeks to present the value of the net gains or losses in total social resources associated with each participant's program experience and its effects. It addresses the question of whether society gains or loses goods and services as a result of the supported work program. In the social perspective, transfer payments that redistribute income among different groups in society (e.g., welfare payments) are not counted as benefits or losses, because they involve no change in overall resources.[2] However, such payments do enter into the participants' perspective, which looks at the gains and losses to the supported worker, and the nonparticipant perspective, which sees all program operating expenses as costs and welfare savings as benefits.

From the social perspective, supported work's costs include all the expense of operating the local programs, with the exception of supported workers' wages. Other costs include the administrative cost to the Manpower Demonstration Research Corporation (MDRC) for monitoring local operations and giving them technical assistance, the output the participants would have produced had they not been employed in supported work, and additional child care costs related to the AFDC women's increased employment.

2. Reductions in welfare administrative costs that accompany a decline in benefits are, however, a social benefit.

Social benefits include the output produced by the supported workers while they are in the program; increases in their post-program earnings; reductions in criminal activities; and savings from reduced participation in other employment, training, or drug treatment programs. Estimates of the value of in-program output were based on the detailed examination of a sample of 44 work projects at sites with random assignment. Estimates of the program's impact on employment and other behavior were based on comparisons of the activities of experimentals and controls as reported in interviews with the research sample. For the employment results, the earnings data could be used directly. To assess program impact on criminal activity, the benchmark estimate was arrived at from arrest data collected in interviews with participants, which were then adjusted to offset underreporting. The adjustment was based on a comparison of data provided in the interviews with police arrest records for a sample of individuals. The benchmark calculation was further refined by separate estimates of reductions in property damage and personal injury, stolen property, and criminal justice system costs.

Developing an estimate of the supported work demonstration's behavioral impacts over time (and most critically for earnings and criminal activities where the impacts were the largest) confronted the researchers with two complex analysis tasks: finding an appropriate number to represent the demonstration-wide impacts for months 19 through 36,[3] for which information was available only for certain subsets (cohorts) of the sample; and estimating the extent to which impacts observed during those months would extend into the future.

Estimations for Months 19 through 36
As discussed previously, the supported work data suggests that employment impacts were largest for the early enrollees—the group whom researchers followed longest. This seems partially a result of the effect that the then continually improving labor market had on the employment opportunities of the control group. Because about 50 to 85 percent of the sample in each target group was assigned a 27-month interview (see Table 3-1), data from that sample were considered sufficiently typical of the overall sample to be used directly in the benefit-cost estimates for those months.[4]

3. Months 19 through 27 for the AFDC sample.
4. For the AFDC group, however, where the 27-month follow-up was given to the smallest share of the total sample, and where it also served as the base for extrapolation because there were no 36-month interviews, one of the sensitivity tests combined the 18-month and 27-month cohorts to derive a lower estimate of program impacts.

However, when it came to the ex-offender, ex-addict, and youth groups in the 28- to 36-month period after random assignment, the sample was judged to be too small to have confidence in it as a base for extrapolating benefits into the future.[5] Instead, a procedure was developed to provide an estimate that was more representative of the experience of the full research sample and that would neither disregard the findings observed for the small 36-month cohort nor give it undue weight in assessing impact on the larger sample. Thus, behavioral changes for this period were based on a weighted average of the 19- to 27-month changes for the 27-month cohort and the 28- to 36-month changes for the 36-month cohort. In addition, sensitivity tests examine whether the results would differ under more generous or conservative assumptions.

Extrapolation

Most costs occur while participants are enrolled in supported work, but benefits extend into future years. Even though extrapolation involves some degree of inherent uncertainty and the need for some nonquantifiable judgments, a realistic analysis cannot make the extreme assumption that there is no programmatic impact after the last interview. Thus, a number of assumptions were adopted to develop the benchmark estimates of future benefits, and the impact of alternative assumptions examined in sensitivity tests. First, the 28- to 36-month weighted average impacts (and the 19 to 27-month impacts for the AFDC women) were used as the base for extrapolation. Second, benefits were assumed to extend over the period of a typical working life, as provided in population tables. Next, relying primarily on one of the few studies of the long-term impacts of employment programs, benefits were assumed to decay over time from the base period values at a rate of 50 percent every five years for the ex-addicts, ex-offenders and youth, and to continue nominally unchanged for the AFDC women.[6] Finally, all benefits and costs beyond the initial 9-month period were converted into present values on the basis of a real (i.e., inflation adjusted) discount rate of 5 percent per year.

5. Of those groups, 33 percent of the ex-addicts, 22 percent of the ex-offenders, and 16 percent of the youths were assigned these interviews.

6. This is based on a study by Orley Ashenfelter of participants in the MDTA program. See Orley Ashenfelter, "Estimating the Effect of Training Programs on Earnings," *Review of Economics and Statistics*, LX (1978): 47–57. The benchmark assumptions on the decay of nominal earnings are equivalent to a 3 percent per year decay in real earnings differentials for the AFDC women and a 17 percent per year decay in real earnings for the other target groups.

Unmeasured Costs and Benefits

Even this complex methodology could not cover all program effects. For example, the estimates do not include the psychological benefits of employment ot the supported workers, or of the reduction of criminal activity to society. Nor do the estimates include as a benefit the extent to which supported work fulfills society's clear preference for providing employment for youth and substituting work for welfare or other transfer payments as the source of income for disadvantaged people. In addition, there is no quantification of the benefits to the children and other family members that accompany the increased employment of the supported workers both during and after the program. There is also no estimate of the possible benefits or losses to the children of AFDC women that may result from different types of child care associated with their mothers' going to work. Finally, there is no assessment of the possible indirect effects of supported work on the total labor force—either the negative effects of displacement or the positive effects of an increased demand for low-skilled labor.

Some of these effects may be quite significant, and many of them are likely to be beneficial. Therefore, the data on measured benefits and costs presented in this chapter should be considered only a partial balance sheet. A more complete judgment of supported work will require an assessment of the importance of these additional unmeasured benefits.

THE BENEFIT-COST FINDINGS

AFDC Women

The first column of Table 8-1 summarizes the social benefits and costs during the first 27 months after random assignment, a period that includes nearly all of the program costs but not the full post-program benefits. The benefit-cost data for these first 27 months are particularly reliable, because they come directly from the experimental-control interviews and do not require extrapolation assumptions. Overall, the social benefits during this period are substantial ($5,818) and come close to offsetting the social costs for each supported worker ($6,606). The largest benefit is the value of the output produced by each AFDC woman while in supported work ($4,520), which about equals the wages received by the women for their work in the program.[7] Additional benefits

---

7. The average AFDC woman received $4,856 in earnings and fringe benefits from the supported work program. Table 8-1, which is limited to social costs, does not include supporter worker wages, which are benefits to the participants, costs to the nonparticipants, and of no cost to society. This relationship between value of output and wages holds for all four target groups.

Table 8-1. Summary of Social Benefits and Costs per Participant: AFDC Target Group

Item	Months 1-27	Total
Benefits		
Value of in-program output	$4,520	$4,520
Increased post-program earnings	1,028	9,193
Reduced welfare system administrative costs	137	811
Reduced education and employment program costs	133	608
Total	$5,818	$15,132
Costs		
Local supported work program costs[a]	-$5,105	-$5,105
MDRC central administrative costs	-270	-270
Foregone earnings of participants	-879	-879
Increased child care costs	-352	-728
Total	-$6,606	-$6,982
Net present value (benefits minus costs)	-$ 787	$8,150
Range of alternative estimates of net present value	n.a.	$2,754 to $9,732

Source: Peter Kemper, David Long, and Craig Thornton, *The Supported Work Evaluation: The Final Benefit-Cost Analysis* (New York: MDRC, 1980).

Notes: To correct for inflation, all dollar values have been measured in terms of fourth-quarter 1976 dollars. They have also been discounted (at a 5 percent annual rate) to the midpoint of the first 9-month period. Numbers may not sum due to rounding.

[a]Including the cost of operating the work projects (e.g., supervision, materials, and equipment) and of program overhead, but excluding supported work wages.

flow from the increase in post-program earnings during this period ($1,028).

Even though a net cost of $787 remains after 27 months, the net present value becomes positive when extrapolated future benefits are included. The benchmark estimates presented in Table 8-1 show that supported work generates an estimated $8,150 more in resources per participant than it uses up, primarily as a result of the assumed continued difference in the earnings of the experimentals compared to the controls.

As outlined earlier, these benchmark estimates were derived by the Mathematica researchers' use of their best judgment on a number of critical factors affecting the value of extrapolated benefits and cost and other assumptions. In addition, the benefit-cost study included a number of alternative estimates that place net benefits between $2,754 and $9,732, depending on each assumption:[8]

1. The program impacts during the base period (months 19 through 27) and for the future were assumed to be lower, based on an average of the findings for the 27-month and 18-month cohorts (net present value = $5,506).[9]
2. The program benefits were assumed to decay at a faster rate (50 percent in 5 years) (net present value = $2,754).
3. Alternative "real" discount rates (3 and 10 percent) were used in estimating the net present value of benefits and costs (net present value = $9,732 or $4,639).
4. A much more conservative approach was adopted in valuing in-program output (net present value = $6,106).

The range of net present value estimates suggests both caution and confidence. Despite the unusually extensive information available for this study, different values within the range indicate that the reader should be careful not to attach particular importance to any one number, but focus on the general trend of the findings. However, the fact that the overall qualitative conclusion—that is, the positive sign of the net present value estimates—remains unaffected by the wide range of alternative assumptions points to the strength of the findings for this target group.

The preceding paragraphs present the benefit-cost results from the perspective of society as a whole. The benefits were also positive from the more limited perspectives of the supported work participants themselves and the rest of society, the nonparticipating tax-

8. Researchers conducted other sensitivity tests, but they were not included in the ranges of Table 8–1 because they were considered extreme (e.g., assuming no benefits occur after months 27 or 36) or particularly speculative (e.g., specifying the extent of the displacement of other workers by supported workers). This fuller analysis is contained in forthcoming more detailed reports.

9. The benchmark estimate uses the earnings and other impacts found for the 27-month cohort both for the 19- through 27-month period and as the base for extrapolating future benefits. However, this sensitivity test takes a more conservative approach, based on the indication discussed in Chapter 4 that supported work's impacts during months 16–18 were smaller for the 18-month cohort than for the 27-month cohort. For this estimate, the base period for extrapolation of post-program earnings is the weighted average of the month 16 through 18 earnings difference for the 18-month cohort and the 19 through 27-month difference for the 27-month cohort. This procedure is similar to that used in developing the 28–36 month base period figure included in the benchmark estimates for the other three target groups. For the AFDC group, however, it is presented as a sensitivity test rather than included in the benchmark estimate out of a concern that the data for months 16–18 are from a period too early to provide a sufficiently reliable estimate of post-program effects.

payers. Critical to this latter group are the reductions in AFDC, Medicaid, and other transfer payments that are associated with the increased earnings of the supported work experimentals. Even though these did not show up as benefits in the broader social perspective (because they are gains to the nonparticipants and losses to the participants), they become major considerations when the two groups are examined separately. Taxpayer savings from reductions in these transfer payments total an estimated $2,615 during the first 27 months after an AFDC participant enrolls in supported work and over $10,000 when future savings are extrapolated, using the same method as was applied to earnings. In addition, the nonparticipants benefit from the increased taxes paid by the AFDC women as they move from welfare to a job. When these two savings are combined with the program's other benefits, the nonparticipating taxpayers' gains far outweigh their costs (the benchmark estimate shows a difference of over $8,000).[10]   Finally, supported work also appears to yield net benefits to the participants, primarily as a result of their increased earnings both in and after the program, although these earnings gains were largely offset by reductions in welfare payments.

Ex-Addicts

As Table 8–2 indicates, the social benefits also exceed the costs for the ex-addicts, although the reasons for this outcome are quite different from those that account for the results of the AFDC group. Over the 27-month period for which the most reliable data are available, the consistent and large reduction in criminal activities, when combined with the value of in-program output ($3,363) and other smaller changes, brings total benefits to within $215 of total costs. Thus, only a modest amount of additional benefits is required from the post-27-month period (when the analysis relies on the small sample and the extrapolation approach) for total benefits to exceed costs. Furthermore, the long-term follow-up data (as shown in Chapter 5) suggest that benefits from both reduced criminal activities and increased earnings occur during months 28 through 36. Even when these are extrapolated using the weighted average approach outlined above, the additional benefits are substantial and bring benchmark estimates of total social benefits $4,345 above total social costs. In contrast to the AFDC findings, the positive

10. The full report on the benefit-cost analysis presents the detailed components of benefits and costs under these two perspectives, as well as the sensitivity of these estimates to changes in the particular assumptions used to estimate different items.

Table 8-2. Summary of Social Benefits and Costs per Participant: Ex-Addict Target Group

Item	Months 1-27	Total
Benefits		
Value of in-program output	$3,363	$3,363
Increased post-program earnings	-153	819
Reduced welfare system administrative costs	47	-64
Reduced criminal activities[a]	1,677	5,178
Reduced drug treatment costs	-3	153
Reduced education and employment program costs	72	114
Total	$5,003	$9,563
Costs		
Local supported work program costs[b]	-$3,798	-$3,798
MDRC central administrative costs	-201	-201
Foregone earnings of participants	-1,219	-1,219
Total	-$5,218	-$5,218
Net present value (benefits minus costs)	-$215	$4,345
Range of alternative estimates of net present value	n.a.	$172 to $10,777

Source: Peter Kemper, David Long, and Craig Thornton, *The Supported Work Evaluation: The Final Benefit-Cost Analysis* (New York: MDRC, 1980).
Notes: To correct for inflation, all dollar values have been measured in terms of fourth-quarter 1976 dollars. They have also been discounted (at a 5 percent annual rate) to the midpoint of the first 9-month period. Numbers may not sum due to rounding.
[a]Including reduced judicial system costs, reduced personal injury and property damage, and reduced stolen property.
[b]Including the cost of operating the work projects (e.g., supervision, materials and equipment) and of program overhead, but excluding supported worker wages.

net present value for the ex-addicts is primarily the result of reduced criminal activities rather than of increased post-program earnings; in contrast to the ex-offender results, the ex-addict changes in criminal activities are stable over the full period of observation and thus can be confidently included in the benchmark benefit-cost calculation.

The range of alternative estimates for the ex-addict group given in Table 8-2 reflects the following assumptions:

1. Real discount rates of 3 or 10 percent (net present value = $4,994 or $3,155).
2. A lower decay rate similar to that used in the benchmark AFDC estimate (net present value = $10,777).

3. The use of either the 27-month or 36-month cohort as the exclusive base for extrapolation (net present value = $172 or $9,392).
4. The use of a sharply lower estimate of the benefit of the reduction in criminal activities (net present value = $1,755).
5. A lower value of output (net present value = $2,824).

The low value of the range ($172) is a relatively extreme estimate based solely on the 27-month cohort, and thus ignoring the significant earnings increase and crime reduction observed for the 36-month cohort. The upper bound is based on a similarly unlikely assumption for this group, namely, that the impact observed in the base period does not decay in future years. Although the range of estimates is large, it is important to note that for the ex-addicts, as for the AFDC group, the qualitative conclusion that social benefits exceed costs remains unchanged under all of these alternative assumptions.[11] In addition, benefits are substantial and positive from the complementary perspective of the ex-addict participants and nonparticipants. (The benchmark estimates are $3,076 and $1,268, respectively.)

Youths

In contrast to the AFDC and ex-addict findings, the benefits of supported work fall short of the costs for the youth target group (see Table 8-3). Despite the substantial benefits from the value of output produced while the youths are employed in the program ($3,394), the absence of any impact on criminal activities or subsequent employment leads to an overall net social cost of $1,465. Under a range of alternative assumptions identical to those tested for the ex-addicts, this estimate varies widely, but the conclusion is consistently negative. However, from the perspective of the participating youths, the program does have benefits (redistributing an estimated $892 per youth), whereas from the perspective of nonparticipants there are net costs of $2,357 per youth.

Although the range of estimates suggests that the measured social costs are likely to exceed the benefits, a consideration of unmeasured benefits may be particularly appropriate for this group. Clearly, as evidenced in the recent large number of youth employment pro-

---

11. In addition to the sensitivity test shown in the range in Table 8-2, the full analysis also provides more extreme estimates (e.g., no benefits from the reduction in criminal activities) under which the social costs for ex-addicts would exceed the benefits. Because of their extreme quality, however, these have been excluded from the Table 8-2 range.

Table 8–3. Summary of Social Benefits and Costs per Participant: Youth Target Group

Item	Months 1–27	Total
Benefits		
Value of in-program output	$3,394	$3,394
Increased post-program earnings	-3	29
Reduced welfare system administrative costs	78	228
Reduced criminal activities[a]	103	-89
Reduced drug treatment costs	-26	-116
Reduced education and employment program costs	87	100
Total	$3,633	$3,546
Costs		
Local supported work program costs[b]	-$3,833	-$3,833
MDRC central administrative costs	-203	-203
Foregone earnings of participants	-974	-974
Total	-$5,010	-$5,010
Net present value (benefits minus costs)	-$1,377	-$1,465
Range of alternative estimates of net present value	n.a.	-$4,118 to -$ 250

Source: Peter Kemper, David Long, and Craig Thornton, *The Supported Work Evaluation: The Final Benefit-Cost Analysis* (New York: MDRC, 1980).
Notes: To correct for inflation, all dollar values have been measured in terms of fourth-quarter 1976 dollars. They have also been discounted (at a 5 percent annual rate) to the midpoint of the first 9-month period. Numbers may not sum due to rounding.
[a]Including reduced judicial system costs, reduced personal injury and property damage, and reduced stolen property.
[b]Including the cost of operating the work projects (e.g., supervision, materials, and equipment) and of program overhead, but excluding supported worker wages.

grams, there is a strong national interest in providing jobs and income for unemployed high school dropouts. Although it is unclear how much society is willing to pay to put a youth to work, the value may be substantial. An overall conclusion on supported work for this group, therefore, would depend both on whether the unmeasured benefit of providing a supported job for each youth exceeded the estimated $1,465 net measured social cost, and on whether this objective could be met at a lower measured cost under alternative employment initiatives. Unfortunately, answers on both questions are not available. The social value of increasing youth employment is uncertain and there is a paucity of reliable estimates of the net social cost of alternative employment programs.

Ex-Offenders

During months 1 through 27, the social costs exceeded the benefits for the ex-offender group by $2,224, the largest amount of the four target groups. However, a large share of this amount is attributable to an increase in criminal activities which, as noted in Chapter 7, was not statistically significant and thus could have occurred by chance. When the results from these months are combined with the extrapolated future benefits, the results are ambiguous. In contrast to the findings for the other three target groups, not only the magnitude but the plus or minus sign of the estimate of net present value depends on the assumptions used in extrapolation. If the estimate is based solely on the subset of the sample followed for 36 months—which had both a substantial increase in employment and a reduction in criminal activities—benefits exceed costs by $8,292. If only the 27-month cohort is used—which had a smaller earnings increase and an increase in criminal activities—costs exceed benefits by $4,916.

An examination of Table 8-4, which shows the components of the estimate under these two extreme extrapolation assumptions, indicates that the wide variation is due primarily to differences in the estimates of criminal activities. This suggests one of the problems of including crime estimates in the benefit-cost framework. Because individual arrests are relatively rare events, each of which has a high social cost, arrests introduce an unstable factor into the analysis. For the ex-addicts, for whom the crime impacts are statistically significant and sustained, this did not create a problem. For the ex-offenders, for whom the measured impacts vary widely over time and among subsets of the sample and are not statistically significant, their inclusion contributes heavily to an uncertain outcome. Because of this, Table 8-4 includes no single benchmark estimate but rather an alternative set of ranges, depending on the inclusion or exclusion of crime effects, and the other sensitivity tests noted above.

Furthermore, Table 8-4 indicates that the uncertainty goes beyond the crime estimates. When criminal activity measures are excluded from the calculation, the range of estimates of net present value is sharply narrowed though still not clearly positive or negative. If all of the other benchmark assumptions are adopted, net present value ranges from -$166 to $1,434, depending on the cohort used as the base for extrapolation. Moreover, if the alternative assumptions on decay and discount rates and value of output that were examined for the other target groups are considered, this range increases to from -$1,654 to $1,434.

For the ex-offenders, the overall demonstration-wide assessment

Table 8-4. Summary of Social Benefits and Costs per Participant: Ex-Offender Target Group

Item	Months 1-27	Total
Benefits		
Value of in-program output	$2,973	$2,973
Increased post-program earnings	304	851 to 2,792[a]
Reduced welfare system administrative costs	41	7 to 310[a]
Reduced criminal activities[b]	-1,048	-4,750 to 6,858[a]
Reduced drug treatment costs	6	389 to -380[a]
Reduced education and employment program costs	136	250 to 374[a]
Total	$2,412	-$ 280 to $12,927[a]
Costs		
Local supported work program costs[c]	-$3,359	-$3,359
MDRC central administrative costs	-178	-178
Foregone earnings of participants	-1,100	-1,100
Total	-$4,637	-$4,637
Net present value (benefits minus costs)	-$2,224	-$4,916 to $8,292[a]
Net present value, excluding changes in criminal activities	-$1,176	- $166 to $1,434[a]
Range of alternative estimates of net present value, excluding changes in criminal activities	n.a.	-$1,654 to $1,434[d]

Source: Peter Kemper, David Long, and Craig Thornton, *The Supported Work Evaluation: The Final Benefit-Cost Analysis* (New York: MDRC, 1980).

Notes: To correct for inflation, all dollar values have been measured in terms of fourth-quarter 1976 dollars. They have also been discounted (at a 5 percent annual rate) to the midpoint of the first 9-month period. Numbers may not sum due to rounding.

[a]This range reflects differences in findings for the 27- and 36-month cohorts. The value for the 27-month cohort appears first, that for the 36-month cohort second. All other benchmark assumptions are employed.

[b]Including reduced judicial system costs, reduced personal injury and property damage, and reduced stolen property.

[c]Including the cost of operating the work projects (e.g., supervision, materials, and equipment) and of program overhead, but excluding supported worker wages.

[d]This range reflects the use of alternative estimates of value of output and decay and discount rates, as well as the benchmark estimate.

of benefits and costs is uncertain. A more complete assessment of the role of supported work for this target group must depend on a judgment about any unmeasured benefits that accompany the employment of ex-offenders.

※ *Chapter 9*

Summary and Conclusions

The preceding chapters reported in detail on the structure of the demonstration and on the findings from the research. This final chapter summarizes the results and discusses their implications and limitations.

SUMMARY OF THE OPERATING EXPERIENCE

The National Supported Work Demonstration was designed to test whether and to what extent 12 to 18 months of employment in a supportive, but performance-oriented, environment would equip some of America's hardest-to-employ people to get and hold normal, unsubsidized jobs. The research focused on four particular disadvantaged groups: ex-offenders and former drug addicts, women who had been long-term recipients of welfare benefits, and young school dropouts, many with a criminal or delinquency record. In order to obtain answers about the program's effectiveness and cost, the program design called for a comprehensive research effort as an integral part of the demonstration. To meet the research requirements, 6,616 eligible applicants at 10 of the 15 sites were randomly assigned either to an experimental group (offered a job in supported work) or to a control group (not offered a job), and were subsequently interviewed at intervals for up to 36 months. A systematic effort was made to assess the program's impacts on earnings and employment, welfare dependency, and drug use and criminal activities. In addition, the analysis was designed to develop estimates of the program's benefits and costs.

The demonstration was implemented by independent local agencies, which were responsible for recruiting workers who met the eligibility criteria; developing and operating worksites on the basis of the demonstration's essential components (peer support, graduated stress, and close supervision); paying salaries at or slightly above the minimum wage; and providing a disciplined work environment, including the promotion, suspension, or termination of supported workers on the basis of their performance. At or before the end of the 12 or 18 months of maximum employment in the program, the local agencies also were to assist supported workers in locating regular employment.

The program's sharply defined eligibility criteria were designed to recruit a group of individuals who had particularly serious difficulties in getting and retaining regular employment. Most supported workers were black or Hispanic. Most of them had not finished high school, had very limited recent work experience, and were heavily dependent on transfer payments. The programs also reached a group of ex-addicts and ex-offenders with a history of drug use, prior arrests, and convictions. These groups averaged a total of 129 and 195 weeks, respectively, of incarceration prior to their enrollment in supported work. A comparison of the characteristics of supported workers with those in positions funded under CETA and the Work Incentive (WIN) program shows that supported work indeed was reaching a more disadvantaged group than the population typically served by other employment programs.

The local supported work agencies created worksites that varied in types of work, customers served, and funding arrangements. Approximately half of the work was in various service activities, over a quarter was in construction, and a substantial amount in manufacturing. About 75 percent of the work was performed for public and nonprofit customers, the other 25 percent for private individuals or firms. Finally, in contrast to the procedures of the CETA programs, the local agencies in most cases charged their customers for the services or products of the supported workers. The emphasis on marketable goods and services had two benefits. It helped to assure that the programs produced outputs that were of value to their communities, and it compelled the local management to operate worksites with a discipline that contributed to a more realistic work experience for the participants.

A review of the operating statistics on all of the approximately 10,000 supported work employees at the 15 sites suggests that the program was most successful with the AFDC group. The AFDC women had the highest attendance rates (90 percent, compared to 84 and 80 percent for the ex-addicts and ex-offenders and the lowest rate of 76 percent for the youths); the longest average time in the program (9.5 months compared to 5 to 7 months for the other three groups); the highest rate of departures to a job (35 percent compared to 23 to 29 percent for the others); and the lowest rage of firings (11 percent, compared to 33 to 37 percent). However, the data also indicate that the AFDC group was highest in mandatory graduations—termination after the full span of the program for individuals who had not been placed in a regular job. This shows that the programs had difficulty developing acceptable jobs for even this relatively successful group of employees. That the program achieved the placement rate it did for the other three target groups is encouraging, given the prior work histories of the participants. At the same time the high rates of firings for these groups show that they included a substantial number who could not or would not meet the work demands of even a supported work job.

The program's fiscal data show that it cost the government about $10,300 to provide a year of supported work employment, which translates into about $5,700 per supported work employee, a figure quite comparable to the average cost of providing public service employment under the CETA program.

The demonstration posed special management challenges arising out of the nature and objectives of supported work. The need to establish job sites with a realistic work environment forced the sites to face many of the challenges of small businesses seeking to market their products. This required flexibility in oversight and funding, along with efforts to make sure that operations were competently managed and did not waste public funds.

A second challenge was posed by the characteristics of the target population. The supported work sites faced the opposing goals embodied in much recent employment legislation: to recruit the least promising employees and yet to hold down operating costs and meet high performance standards (e.g., in terms of placement and attendance rates). The inevitable conflict of these objectives was contained during the demonstration by the recognition of a larger interest in serving the target population. Performance and cost standards were viewed as a necessary part of the management and monitoring process, but it was realized that excessive reliance on these criteria would push the sites toward "creaming" the most employable applicants. And if that had happened, the very purpose of the demonstration would have been undermined.

SUMMARY OF THE RESEARCH FINDINGS
ON PROGRAM IMPACT AND COST

The supported work research findings suggest that the program was generally successful in meeting its short-term objectives of increasing employment and earnings, reducing welfare dependency, and producing useful goods and services. For two of the target groups—AFDC women and ex-addicts—it also succeeded in producing long-term impacts. In addition, the benefits for these two groups were considerably in excess of costs. For the other two target groups, there is little indication of any long-term impacts, and the negative or ambiguous findings from the benefit-cost analysis suggest that ultimate judgments about these groups will depend on the significance of unmeasured benefits.

THE AFDC TARGET GROUP

Both when measured by operational data and when compared to the control group, supported work was most successful with the group of long-term AFDC recipients. As Table 9–1 shows, participation in supported work led to an increase in employment and a reduction in welfare dependency, both while the AFDC group was in the program and after it had left it. The impacts were largest during the first 9 months, when most of the experimentals had a supported work job, but continued at statistically significant levels into the 19- to 27-month post-program period. The more detailed data presented in Chapter 4 show that after month 16 there was no further decline in the program's impact, suggesting that supported work had a durable impact on employment behavior. (This will be further examined in a report on a supplemental wave of follow-up interviews with AFDC experimentals and controls, to be completed in late 1980.) A comparison of the data in Table 9–1 on the employment rates, hours, and earnings show that the experimentals were not only employed more often but that those who were employed worked more hours at higher wages, suggesting that supported work also helped its participants find jobs of a higher quality.

Examination of the behavior among subgroups within the AFDC population suggested that supported work's impact was particularly large for older women (those between 36 and 44 years old at the time of enrollment), and for women who had never worked before, or had been on welfare longest. In contrast, subgroups which did relatively well in the absence of the program (e.g., those with 12 or

Table 9-1. Experimental-Control Differences in Key Indicators during the 27 Months Following Enrollment: AFDC Target Group

Outcome Measure	Experimentals	Controls	Difference
Percent employed during period			
Months 1–9	96.3	36.5	59.8†
10–18	76.5	39.4	37.1†
19–27	49.1	40.6	8.5†
Average monthly hours worked			
Months 1–9	135.3	26.6	108.7†
10–18	79.4	40.3	39.1†
19–27	60.9	45.2	15.7†
Average monthly earnings ($)			
Months 1–9	400.44	78.28	322.16†
10–18	274.06	131.08	142.98†
19–27	242.89	165.88	77.01†
Cash welfare payments[a]			
Percent receiving			
Months 1–9	93.8	97.7	-3.9†
10–18	82.4	90.1	-7.7†
19–27	71.4	85.1	-13.7†
Average monthly amount ($)			
Months 1–9	169.82	277.90	-108.09†
10–18	164.28	246.60	-82.32†
19–27	172.06	224.00	-51.94†
Food stamps: average monthly bonus value ($)			
Months 1–9	44.83	63.46	-18.63†
10–18	42.15	58.02	-15.87†
19–27	47.14	60.25	-13.11†
Average monthly total income[b]($)			
Months 1–9	628.06	435.10	192.96†
10–18	524.47	454.44	70.03†
19–27	497.50	470.14	27.36

Source: See Table 4–1.
Notes: Averages are calculated for all members of the sample, including those with no employment or transfer payment receipt in the covered period.
[a]Welfare includes AFDC, GA, SSI, and other unspecified cash welfare.
[b]Total income includes earnings, unemployment compensation, welfare, food stamp bonus value, and other unearned income (Social Security, pensions, alimony, and child support).
†Statistically significant at the 5 percent level.

more years of schooling) seemed to have been less affected by participation in the program.

As a result of their higher earnings, the AFDC participants received substantially less income from the AFDC and food stamp programs. Over the 27-month period followed in the interviews, experimentals received a total of $2,600 less in benefits from these two programs. By months 19 through 27, about twice as many experimentals as controls had left the AFDC rolls.

The supported work findings confirm that this group often works despite substantial disincentives. Because welfare benefits are reduced as earnings increase, the experimental-control differentials in total income are much less than those in earnings. When all offsetting changes are considered (those in Social Security and other taxes, Medicaid, and other in-kind benefits), the real income of the AFDC experimentals and controls increases by less than 50 cents for each dollar earned.

The results of the benfit-cost analysis suggest that the program generates substantially more resources per AFDC participant than it uses up. The researchers' best guess or benchmark estimate is that the estimated social benefits for this group exceed the costs by a total of $8,150 per participant. Alternative nonextreme assumptions about critical benefit-cost components or approaches produced a range of estimates: $2,754 to $9,732. The range suggests that emphasis be placed not on a single number but rather on the general direction of findings; the consistently positive outcome under widely varying assumptions suggests the strength of the benefit-cost results for this target group.

When the focus of the benefit-cost analysis is shifted from society as a whole to the nonparticipants (often called the taxpayers) the data suggest that, from this more limited perspective too, the investment in supported work more than pays for itself, with benefits exceeding costs by a large amount, primarily as a result of the savings in welfare payments.

THE EX-ADDICT TARGET GROUP

During the early months after random assignment, when the ex-addict participants were still in the program, there were substantial differentials in employment, hours, and earnings between the participants (experimentals) and the control group (see Table 9–2). After a decline in the experimental-control differentials, during months 16 to 30, there was a reversal, with significant differences in the employment indicators during months 31 through 36. Clearly, for the sample of ex-addicts that were followed the full 36 months, supported work had substantial long-term employment impacts. However, the reasons for the upturn and the magnitude of the effect that would have been found had the whole sample been followed for 36 months are uncertain. The shorter term follow-up data on the individuals who enrolled in the program at a later date, when the controls experienced greater employment opportunities, suggest that the program impacts were smaller. To further clarify

Table 9-2. Experimental-Control Differences in Key Indicators during the 36 Months Following Enrollment: Ex-Addict Target Group

Outcome Measure	Experimentals	Controls	Difference
Percent employed during period			
Months 1-9	95.0	50.2	44.8†
10-18	63.9	53.1	10.8†
19-27	56.5	53.0	3.5
28-36	64.0	53.9	10.1*
Average monthly hours worked			
Months 1-9	118.7	40.5	78.2†
10-18	66.4	50.0	16.4†
19-27	60.1	58.6	1.5
28-36	70.9	52.6	18.3†
Average monthly earnings ($)			
Months 1-9	361.23	159.79	201.44†
10-18	259.62	220.42	39.20*
19-27	277.75	261.33	16.42
28-36	326.09	224.36	101.73†
Average monthly welfare and food stamps benefits ($)[a]			
Months 1-9	57.97	115.17	-57.20†
10-18	92.42	110.89	-18.47†
19-27	89.90	93.94	-4.04
28-36	94.34	103.79	-9.45
Percent using any drug other than marijuana or alcohol			
Months 1-9	36.1	38.2	-2.1
10-18	34.1	32.7	1.4
19-27	28.0	27.5	0.5
28-36	23.4	20.7	2.7
Percent using heroin			
Months 1-9	20.2	21.5	-1.3
10-18	16.8	17.8	-1.0
19-27	13.4	11.7	1.7
28-36	10.1	8.8	1.3
Percent arrested			
Months 1-18	25.3	33.5	-8.2†
1-36	35.0	53.1	-18.1†
Percent arrested for robbery			
Months 1-18	2.3	7.5	-5.2†
1-36	0.2	13.4	-13.2†
Percent arrested on drug charges			
Months 1-18	4.1	7.9	-3.8†
1-36	6.8	14.0	-7.2
Percent convicted			
Months 1-18	13.5	17.8	-4.3*
1-36	19.3	32.9	-13.6*

Source: See Tables 5-1 and 5-8.

Notes: Averages are calculated for all members of the sample, including those with no employment or transfer payment receipt in the covered period.

[a]Welfare includes AFDC, GA, SSI, and other unspecified cash welfare. These data are based on a sample slightly different from that in Table 5-5.

†Statistically significant at the 5 percent level.

*Statistically significant at the 10 percent level.

the long-term employment impacts and their dependence on labor market conditions, it would be useful to conduct a supplemental follow-up of this sample, probably using the relatively inexpensive means of tracing earnings through Social Security records.[1]

Second, and probably most critical, supported work participation resulted in a sharp reduction in the criminal activities of the ex-addict group. As shown in Table 9–2, during the first 18 months after random assignment, there was a 24 percent reduction in the arrest rate for experimentals, 25.3 percent compared to 33.5 percent. Although the differences are concentrated in the in-program period, they extend into the period when the experimentals are no longer in supported work, with a total of 35 percent of the experimentals arrested over the full 36 months compared to 53 percent of the controls. The program was particularly effective in reducing robbery and drug-related arrests, suggesting that, given the absence of a program effect on drug use in general, the program led to the substitution of legitimate for illegitimate income for the purchase of drugs. Finally, the impact on arrests seems to have been particularly large for the older ex-addicts.

For the ex-addicts as for the AFDC women, the benefit-cost analysis shows that society as a whole, and the participants and nonparticipants viewed separately, benefit from the investment in supported work. (The benchmark net present value is $4,345; the range, $172 to $10,777.) The major social benefit for this target group follows from the reduction in criminal activities. While post-program earning changes contribute a small amount, they are dwarfed by the social value of the estimated crime reduction. The other substantial benefit was the value of output the ex-addicts produced while in the program. As was the case for the AFDC group, the positive findings held up under a wide variety of different assumptions about the individual components of the analysis.

THE YOUTH TARGET GROUP

A comparison of the activities of the youth target group in supported work and its control group counterpart indicates that only in the initial period, while the experimentals were in the program, did supported work have an impact on employment and earnings. After that, both as a result of the movement of the experimentals out of the program and the increasing employment of the control

1. An analysis using Social Security records suggested the feasibility of these data as a follow-up source for earnings information for the supported work target groups.

group, there is a rapid decay in program impact (see Table 9-3). An examination of the program's effectiveness among different subgroups of youths suggests that the program may be more successful with youths under 19 years of age, those with one or more dependents to support, those raised in intact families, and those with particularly limited work experience.

An examination of the program's impacts on drug use and criminal activities for this group indicates no overall impact on the former and only a weak suggestion that the program might have a cumulative effect on criminal activities. There is no evidence that supported work led to an increase in the return to school of this population.

The analysis of supported work's social benefits and costs suggests that, under most reasonable assumptions, the program has a net cost. However, the substantial value of in-program output produced by each youth goes a long way toward offsetting costs and brings the benchmark estimate of net present value to -$1,465 per youth. (The range of alternative estimates is -$4,118 to -$250.) An ultimate decision on the appropriateness of supported work for youths would depend on issues beyond the ken of this report—on the extent to which society values the employment and redistributive impacts of the program and on the extent to which supported work is more effective than other programs in achieving these objectives.

THE EX-OFFENDER TARGET GROUP

A comparison of the behavior of the experimental and control groups suggests that supported work had only limited impact on the ex-offender group. The data suggest strong in-program impacts on employment and earnings which decay rapidly during months 10 through 27. For the small sample followed during months 28 through 36 after random assignment, there is an indication that the program has an impact on earnings, although this differential is not statistically significant (see Table 9-4). Finally, there are no overall impacts on criminal activities and drug use.

In contrast to the other three target groups, for the ex-offenders both the overall direction and magnitude of the benefit-cost findings prove to be extremely sensitive to the specific assumptions adopted in the analysis, especially as it relates to the measure of future criminal activities. For the small sample for which 28- 36-month data are available, supported work leads to a large reduction in criminal activities (as well as the substantial increase in the earnings differential noted above). The larger sample, for which only 27 months of data are available, does not show such a trend. Depend-

Table 9-3. Experimental-Control Differences in Key Indicators during the 36 Months Following Enrollment: Youth Target Group

Outcome Measure	Experimentals	Controls	Difference
Percent employed during period			
Months 1-9	98.1	52.5	45.6†
10-18	68.9	62.7	6.2*
19-27	62.6	62.6	0.0
28-36	74.9	66.2	8.7
Average monthly hours worked			
Months 1-9	120.4	39.7	80.7†
10-18	69.9	58.2	11.7†
19-27	68.8	68.2	0.6
28-36	88.6	81.4	7.2
Average monthly earnings ($)			
Months 1-9	350.68	123.95	226.73†
10-18	235.96	205.25	30.71
19-27	268.28	248.98	19.30
28-36	301.05	342.58	-41.53
Average monthly welfare and food stamp benefits ($)[a]			
Months 1-9	31.09	40.86	-9.77†
10-18	32.08	48.66	-16.58†
19-27	46.53	54.09	-7.56
28-36	44.45	54.57	-10.12
Percent using any drug (other than marijuana or alcohol)			
Months 1-9	11.3	14.2	-2.9
10-18	10.5	10.2	0.3
19-27	11.0	10.6	0.4
28-36	16.8	11.0	5.8
Percent using heroin			
Months 1-9	4.0	3.6	0.4
10-18	1.7	2.4	-0.7
19-27	1.8	1.2	0.6
28-36	1.9	1.0	0.9
Percent arrested			
Months 1-18	26.7	27.0	-0.3
1-27[b]	30.5	39.3	-8.8*
Percent convicted			
Months 1-18	16.5	16.0	0.5
1-27[b]	19.6	23.6	-4.0†

Source: See Tables 7-1 and 7-8.

Notes: Averages are calculated for all members of the sample, including those with no employment or transfer payment receipt in the covered period.

[a]Welfare includes AFDC, GA, SSI, and other unspecified cash welfare. These data are based on a sample slightly different from that in Table 6-5.

[b]Data for months 1-27 have been used because data for months 1-36 are based on an unreliably small sample.

†Statistically significant at the 5 percent level.

*Statistically significant at the 10 percent level.

ing on which data are used as the base for extrapolation, social benefits fall short of costs by $4,916 or exceed them by $8,292. Finally, even when changes in criminal activity are excluded from the analysis, the range of estimates is substantial and does not indicate a clear finding. As a result, no single benefit-cost benchmark estimate is presented for this group. Instead, alternative ranges of estimates, depending on the assumptions used and the handling of the crime impacts, have been made.

To obtain further clarification of the program's long-term impact on criminal activities and earnings—and thus on the net social cost—further follow-up using arrest data and Social Security records is suggested. Both methods were utilized as part of the supported work evaluation and turned out to be relatively inexpensive ways to trace the program's impacts of specific areas.

* * *

In assessing the implications of the findings presented in this report, we find several considerations that bear noting. First, while the supported work findings relate to broad social policy questions in areas such as welfare reform, youth employment, targeting of resources, and decriminalization of drug use, this report is not intended to consider what these policies should be. Rather it is intended to add to the base of knowledge for those concerned with developing policies on such issues. Second, while the research was both extensive and comprehensive, as with any attempt to apply social science techniques to assessing human behavior and response, many research questions remain unanswered.

For example, it would have been of great utility to include an analysis of the relative efficacy of supported work as compared to alternative employment and training approaches. Unfortunately, there is little if any comparable research data available on other programs. Therefore, even though the supported work research provides reliable data on the impact and cost of providing a structured employment opportunity, and as such takes a highly important step toward increasing our knowledge on the impact of employment interventions for the disadvantaged, it does not answer the question of whether supported work is more or less effective than other program alternatives.

It would also have been useful to pinpoint with greater clarity the specific features of supported work that led to its relative success or failure. In fact, the demonstration's research included a rigorous and sophisticated quantitative study directed at determining which features of the supported work model contributed most to

Table 9–4. Experimental-Control Differences in Key Indicators during the 36 Months Following Enrollment: Ex-Offender Target Group

Outcome Measure	Experimentals	Controls	Difference
Percent employed during period			
Months 1–9	95.9	58.7	37.2†
10–18	66.0	59.2	6.8†
19–27	56.5	53.3	3.2
28–36	59.0	57.8	1.2
Average monthly hours worked			
Months 1–9	117.1	46.0	71.1†
10–18	66.3	57.8	8.5†
19–27	59.8	60.0	-0.2
28–36	75.0	66.8	8.2
Average monthly earnings ($)			
Months 1–9	378.74	178.38	200.36†
10–18	285.99	260.83	25.16
19–27	269.17	254.18	14.99
28–36	366.80	304.20	62.60
Average monthly welfare and food stamp benefits ($)[a]			
Months 1–9	28.50	48.49	-19.99†
10–18	41.43	60.86	-19.43†
19–27	51.37	50.37	1.00
28–36	51.74	52.96	-1.22
Percent using any drug (other than marijuana or alcohol)			
Months 1–9	30.0	34.2	-4.2*
10–18	26.0	29.0	-3.0
19–27	22.8	24.1	-1.3
28–36	17.0	28.2	-11.2†
Percent using heroin			
Months 1–9	14.3	14.1	0.2
10–18	8.5	10.8	-2.3
19–27	7.5	7.5	0.0
28–36	4.6	8.4	-3.8
Percent arrested			
Months 1–18	47.2	46.2	1.0
1–36	56.8	64.8	-8.0
Percent convicted			
Months 1–18	25.4	26.4	-1.0
1–36	43.9	35.4	8.5

Source: See Tables 7–1 and 7–2.

Notes: Averages are calculated for all members of the sample, including those with no employment or transfer payment receipt in the covered period.

[a]Welfare includes AFDC, GA, SSI, and other unspecified cash welfare. These data are based on a sample slightly different from that in Table 7–5.

†Statistically significant at the 5 percent level.

*Statistically significant at the 10 percent level.

positive program outcomes. This effort yielded very limited insights, and indicates the extreme difficulty of doing quantitative process research on an operating program, even in a relatively controlled environment. Understanding which features of the supported work model deserve modification, expansion, or abandonment must still come largely from qualitative observation and judgment.

It must also be remembered that research on the demonstration did not take place in a vacuum. Alternative programs and services were available to both experimentals and controls, and at times—as in the case of rapidly expanded resources for youth programs and the unexpected availability of special employment insurance—may have limited supported work's potential for impact. The economy and employment conditions generally improved considerably during the course of the demonstration. A different environment could very well have altered the results, and clearly future changes will likely affect future program impacts.

The operating environment of the demonstration also no doubt affected its outcomes. The findings were derived from 15 sites functioning within uniform demonstration guidelines, under the active oversight and control of a management agency. Any expansion of supported work will have to consider how the key features of the program model, particularly its structuring of the work experience, its targeting on the severely disadvantaged, and its operation of revenue-producing worksites, can be preserved and implemented in a nondemonstration climate.

Finally, the uninterrupted flow of referrals to the program—adequate to provide two people for each job over a period of several years—suggests that among the severely disadvantaged there is a strong interest in work, even in jobs that are temporary and pay only slightly more than the minimum wage. The successes of the program with this clientele, though encouraging, were partial. There are a large number of individuals who volunteered for participation but for one reason or another did not gain regular employment after program completion. They remain the severely disadvantaged. Their voluntary attempt at supported work, and failure, points up the continuing need for creative and deliberate programmatic interventions to improve the connection of a small but troubling group of our citizens to the values and activities of the larger American society.

✳

Manpower Demonstration Research Corporation Publications on Supported Work

PUBLISHED REPORTS

Ball, Joseph. IMPLEMENTING SUPPORTED WORK: JOB CREATION STRATEGIES DURING THE FIRST YEAR OF THE NATIONAL DEMONSTRATION, 1977. (Out of print)

Kolan, Nuran, AFL-CIO Appalachian Council. THE WEST VIRGINIA SUPPORTED WORK PROGRAM: A CASE STUDY, 1979.

Manpower Demonstration Research Corporation. FIRST ANNUAL REPORT ON THE NATIONAL SUPPORTED WORK DEMONSTRATION, 1976. (Out of print)

Manpower Demonstration Research Corporation. SECOND ANNUAL REPORT ON THE NATIONAL SUPPORTED WORK DEMONSTRATION, 1978.

Manpower Demonstration Research Corporation. SUMMARY OF THE FIRST ANNUAL REPORT ON THE NATIONAL SUPPORTED WORK DEMONSTRATION, 1976.

Manpower Demonstration Research Corporation. SUMMARY OF THE SECOND ANNUAL REPORT ON THE NATIONAL SUPPORTED WORK DEMONSTRATION, 1978.

Manpower Demonstration Research Corporation. SUMMARY OF THE OPERATING EXPERIENCE AND STATISTICAL HIGHLIGHTS OF THE THIRD YEAR OF THE NATIONAL SUPPORTED WORK DEMONSTRATION, 1979.

Masters, Stanley H. ANALYSIS OF NINE-MONTH INTERVIEWS

FOR SUPPORTED WORK: RESULTS OF AN EARLY SAMPLE, 1977.

Maynard, Rebecca A. ANALYSIS OF NINE-MONTH INTERVIEWS FOR SUPPORTED WORK: RESULTS OF AN EARLY AFDC SAMPLE, 1977.

Maynard, Rebecca A.; Brown, Randall; Schore, Jennifer. THE NATIONAL SUPPORTED WORK DEMONSTRATION: EFFECTS DURING THE FIRST 18 MONTHS AFTER ENROLLMENT, 1979.

Shapiro, Harvey D. WAIVING THE RULES: WELFARE DIVERSION IN SUPPORTED WORK, 1978.

Shapiro, Harvey D. PAYING THE BILLS: A REPORT ON THE ROLE OF LOCAL GRANTS IN FINANCING THE NATIONAL SUPPORTED WORK DEMONSTRATION, 1979.

REPORTS IN PREPARATION

Dickinson, Katherine; Maynard, Rebecca. THE IMPACT OF SUPPORTED WORK ON EX-ADDICTS.

Kemper, Peter; Long, David; Thornton, Craig. THE SUPPORTED WORK EVALUATION: FINAL BENEFIT-COST ANALYSIS.

Masters, Stanley; Maynard, Rebecca. THE IMPACT OF SUPPORTED WORK ON LONG-TERM RECIPIENTS OF AFDC BENEFITS.

Maynard, Rebecca. THE IMPACT OF SUPPORTED WORK ON YOUNG SCHOOL DROPOUTS.

Piliavin, Irving; Gartner, Rosemary. THE IMPACT OF SUPPORTED WORK ON EX-OFFENDERS.

All published reports are available from the Manpower Demonstration Research Corporation at a charge of $3.00 each to handle printing costs and mailing.